From the Darkness of my Mind

By

Ron L. Carter

This book is based on some actual events; however, it has been fictionalized, and all the people and places appearing in it are fiction. Any resemblance to actual places and people, living or dead, is entirely coincidental.

***

Chapter 1 - Introduction

Deep in my mind, I heard someone screaming at what sounded like the top of his lungs. He was crying out in deep pain as he yelled out, "You bitch, you got what you deserved. I hate your fucking guts."

The guard walked by my cell as I woke and said, "Hey Cody, wake up. You're having that crazy dream again." My shirt was soaking wet from sweat, and my throat hurt from the deep thrusting from the strain of my voice. At first, I couldn't tell if I had one of those horrible nightmares or if my present state of mind had left me once again for a short time. I had gone back to that cold, fateful night when I deliberately and brutally took their last breaths.

Since that night, I have often had difficulty separating truth from fiction, but my mind doesn't. It has somehow found a way to separate the two from each other and justify my horrible actions.

The angry part of my brain delighted with my violent and destructive behavior and consistently tried to control me. Somehow, it helped me to cope with what I had done. It kept telling me, "You know you did the right thing, and if you had to do it all over again, you'd do it the same way." That part of my brain felt justified in my every action. I got a lot of satisfaction with what it was saying to me. When it was in control, I didn't have to face or acknowledge the sad and lonely side of how the other part of my brain felt. The other part of my brain felt destroyed and deeply saddened that I had killed someone I loved and cherished.

Smiling, I knew that it would be easy for that part of me to kill again. I felt like it would be just like killing those cats when I was young. After the first one, the rest of them were easy to kill. Sitting there alone, I knew it was a good thing that I was locked up in prison.

The compassionate side of my brain did feel sad that I would never see my family again outside of prison. Still, the practical side of me knew that none of my family ever wanted to see me after the way I had gruesomely tortured the one I loved. The tough side of me knew

I didn't want to have to explain my actions to anyone. Nobody would ever understand what I did anyway. I'm the only one that understood my actions.

While sitting there on the edge of my bunk and thinking back, I could feel the violent part of my brain taking over again as I thought about that night. That part of my brain smothers anything that wasn't dark and angry. I kept hearing deep inside, "Don't fight it. You know they deserved what they got." Caving into the angry side of my brain, I decided to do whatever it wanted from me. Sitting alone in the dark, I said under my breath and gritted my teeth, *"Don't worry, Cody, you already have."*

***

FROM the DARKNESS of my MIND Poem

Deep in my mind, the lightning will strike
I ramble and rage to find what I like
Quivers of time bounce around until they meet
I stumble and fall and leap to my feet
The blood of my love drains from my heart
Withers of pain like a work of art
Love once flowed from my body and soul
But broken halves don't make a whole
I'll forever seek and hope someday, I'll find
That love isn't just a state of mind
Overcome by trivialities, my brain manifests
I'll find out when I'm laid to rest

***

Chapter 2 - Growing Up

My early years are still sketchy as I get bits and pieces back to my memory. The past is like parts of an old movie that bounce around in and out of your head.

I was the oldest of three boys. My brothers were four and six years younger than me, and I didn't hang out with them as we got older or have a very close relationship with them because of the age difference.

My parents didn't get along very well during my early years, and for most of my childhood, I listened to them arguing and fighting over something I thought was stupid. I didn't like being with them from a very early age because of all the ridiculous fighting. My mom always seemed angry with my dad about something, except for the short moments when she allowed him to hug and kiss her when they were alone. She would get physically violent toward him when she wanted her way. At one point in our lives, I can vividly remember my mom going after my dad with a butcher knife and stabbing him a few times. It was so bad that he was hospitalized for three days after getting stitches and almost dying.

Foolishly, it didn't stop my dad from returning to her when he was out of the hospital. I never understood why he let her treat him that way. Maybe her violent behavior was one of the things they fought about, but I always felt she wasn't happy being a wife and a mother. She wanted to be free to do whatever she wanted.

My mom sometimes became abusive toward my brothers and me during those early years. Her favorite punishment for us when she got upset with us was making us go out to the nearest tree, cut off one of the skinny branches, and bring it to her. She would use it to whip us instead of a belt. She would make us get another one if it weren't slim and flexible enough. She liked the thinner ones more than a pencil and the "whippy" ones at the ends. They were the ones that hurt the most.

Sometimes, I would bring her one round and thick, hoping she would use it on me instead of the skinny one. Other times, I would quickly run into my bedroom and put on extra pants and shirts to protect my body. Sometimes, I would grab a book and put it in my pants for additional protection. Nothing worked because she beat me longer and harder once she knew what I did.

She would grab us by one arm and hold us in a death grip away from her body. Once she had a good hold on us, she would start hitting us across the legs. I would immediately start screaming in pain because it hurt so badly. I would start bouncing up and down as soon as she hit me. Unfortunately, that just seemed to make her more frustrated and angrier with me. She would then hit me in the back and arms or wherever the skinny switch could reach. Unfortunately, sometimes, it was across the face. Those tiny switches always left big, hurtful welts wherever they touched my body.

One day, when I was about seven years old, my cousins and I jumped on my bedroom bed. She stormed into my room, yelling at us a few times to stop. When we didn't stop, she returned to the room in a rage. She had one of those skinny switches in her hand. She must've decided she would make an example of me when she grabbed me and started beating me. She was like a crazy person as she grabbed me by the arm and started whipping me right in front of my cousins. She hit me so bad that welts popped up immediately, and blood started oozing out of my body from where the little switch marks met my skin.

It hurt terribly, but I was more embarrassed and angrier that she would do something like that to me right in front of my cousins.

After the beating, I ran crying and hid in my coat closet. I remember crying for hours and repeatedly saying I hated my mom's guts. I was so hurt, both physically and emotionally, over the beating that I wouldn't come out of the closet for two full days and nights except to go to the bathroom and get a drink of water.

For those two days, I curled up in the corner of the closet and cried myself to sleep most of the time. My mom came in several times to check on me and tried apologizing, but I refused to acknowledge her. I felt like she knew she was guilty of beating me too severely and only wanted to comfort herself for what she had done to me.

One day, when I was about twelve years old, she decided to beat me with the switch for something she felt I did wrong. Before the beating, I stopped her and told her that if she hit me, she might as well kill me this time. I told her that if she didn't kill me, it would be the last time she beat me with a switch again. I told her I wouldn't ever stand there and take her wrath. She realized my seriousness because she decided not to whip me that day. That was the last time she threatened to use a switch or raise her hand to beat me. From that point on, she never took her anger out on me.

I didn't know it then, but I figured later in life that she was taking out her anger toward my dad or the fact that she hated her life out on me. It didn't change my feelings about the previous beatings, even after I understood why she did it. I still felt resentment about those beatings for the rest of my life.

I remember most of the many places we lived and how lonely I felt as a young kid. It seemed like my parents were never happy being in the same place for very long, but I think that was just because they weren't pleased with each other and their lives together. I always tried to stay with one of my cousins or grandparents during those days. I wanted to stay away from my parents and their fighting as much as I could.

My dad worked at many migrant jobs because he never had any trade, training, or permanent employment. We were always like gypsies, moving from place to place.

I loved Oklahoma more than any place I'd ever lived, and I called it my home. We went back and forth from Oklahoma to California during my early years because my mom's parents and other family members lived in small towns in California's central valley. I loved visiting my grandparents during my early life because I had a lot to eat, and it was peaceful. Every time we saw them, Grandpa would go back and kill a couple of chickens, and we'd have fried chicken, mashed potatoes and corn, or some other vegetable. It was great because my grandma was a good cook and always made a good feast for us. I loved her meals.

My dad came from a small family with only a brother and a sister, and they lived in Oklahoma. My dad was a good-looking, clean-cut guy about six feet tall, slender, with dark hair. He always wore cowboy boots, Levi's, a long-sleeved shirt, and a cowboy hat. Even though we didn't have much money, he always dressed nicely and carried himself well.

My mom was from a small town in Oklahoma, and she had several brothers and sisters. She was a pretty brunette with a bubbly personality. I felt as though she was always too willing to talk to strangers. Sometimes, she embarrassed me with all her stupid little quirks and the silly things she would say. She was 5' 4" and had a cute, thin figure. Most guys found her beautiful; wherever we went, guys stopped her and flirted. It didn't matter if she had three boys tagging along after her. It always made me angry that some dumb ass she didn't know would stop her and try to talk and flirt with her. She was always willing to talk to them because she loved the attention. Standing and listening to the stupid pick-up lines they used on her was boring. I would roll my eyes as I heard the dummies. When she would turn to walk away, the guys would always stare at her butt. It always made me angry, so I would quickly turn around and spread my legs apart like I was in a gunslinger shootout and then flip them the bird with both hands. Then I would laugh at them because I knew they wouldn't do anything to me. They liked my mom, and she was my protection. I loved doing that to those big, dumb idiots. It always made mom mad that I would flip them off, but it never stopped me.

She tried to teach me right from wrong but wasn't consistent because of her issues and demons. She also wanted to teach me about God by reading the Bible. I believed there was a God when I was young, but I don't know if I thought there was as I got older. I guess you could say I was more of an Agnostic than anything. I believed in a higher power but wasn't sure it was God. However, I didn't do a lot of cursing because it wasn't something I felt I needed to do to make myself look essential or act like a big shot. I cursed only when I got angry about something or with someone. Even though I didn't necessarily believe or not believe in God, I tried not to take His name in vain, just in case He did exist. I didn't want to make Him angry and bring His wrath down on me.

As I got a little older, I remember a lot of separations between my parents. The fighting and splitting up with each other got progressively worse. I would hear them fighting about my dad being with some woman or my mom being with some guy. Unfortunately, that got to the point where it seemed to be their biggest issue. I thought it was ridiculous to fight over something so stupid because being apart caused them to cheat on each other in the first place.

My mom got hooked up with several guys she went out with on dates during their last separation. When my dad found out about them, that was the "last straw" for him. He must've finally just said, that's it, "I've had enough of her," and left. I loved my dad but couldn't get very attached to him because I never knew when he would take off and I would never see him again.

Finally, all my fears came true, and one day, it happened right after my mom's last episode with the two guys. He just left us and never came back. I was around thirteen years old when they finally got a divorce. That's when my entire world turned upside down. I had to grow up fast and felt lost and numb during those next few years. I had to be the man of the house since my dad wasn't around anymore.

***

Chapter 3 - My first kill

After their divorce, mom moved my brothers and me back to Oklahoma, south of Oklahoma City. I don't remember the town's name; it was near the South Canadian River in a rural area. Although I loved my mom, I resented her for the beatings and for not staying with my dad.

Right after we moved there, my mom started going to the local bars at night. Sometimes, she even drove to the larger nearby cities. During that time, she always left me to watch my brothers while she had fun. Sometimes, she would even go into Oklahoma City, and we wouldn't see her until the next day or sometimes two.

One night, when I was only fourteen, she went to one of the bars and left me to watch my brothers as she often did. When she finally got home that night, it was around 2:00 in the morning, and she had a drunk guy with her. She said he had given her a ride home. I could tell they were both drunk when they walked through the door. She was laughing and holding her shoes in her left hand and her right arm around the guy. She was acting stupid, and he was trying to suck on her neck.

As far as I was concerned, he was just another one of those big, sloppy drunk guys she'd met at the bar. She told me he was a traveling salesman from out of state who was spending the night with her. I was very disappointed with her, but this wasn't the first guy she had brought home from the bars. It didn't matter what she did, but I was angry that she got them home.

I met them both at the front door and told them to keep it down that my brothers were sleeping. I also didn't want them to wake up and see what was happening between them. I got in my mom's face and asked her what she was doing with this idiot. When I did that, the guy immediately pushed me out of the way and said, "This doesn't concern you, boy. It's none of your business." I could feel my face flush as the anger and rage quickly went all over my body. I didn't do anything then, but I told myself he had just done the wrong thing. I went back to my room, and while lying clothed on the bed, I started to formulate a plan on what I would do to this big dumb ass. Since my dad wasn't around anymore, I figured I would take care of this big, pushy loudmouth myself.

I could hear them laughing and having sex as the bed banged against the wall in her bedroom. I remember putting my pillow over my head so I didn't have to listen to them. It didn't help because I could still hear what was happening in her bedroom. I hated that helpless feeling I was having as I lay there. It seemed like it lasted for hours when, in truth, it was only a short time. I wasn't happy about my entire encounter with this guy.

I stayed awake until they both fell asleep, and it was in the early morning hours. By then, I had a plan and began to put my thoughts into action. It was about 5:00. I was still dark outside as I quietly crept into my mom's bedroom. I didn't want to wake her, or she would've ruined my entire plan for him.

I went over to the drunken slob, nudged him gently, and whispered into his ear. I told him my mom had come into my room while he was sleeping and told me she wanted him to take me to the store. I told him she would make him breakfast when they woke up. I whispered that she wanted it to be a surprise, so make sure he didn't wake her. He grumbled around for a few minutes and, at first, was very reluctant to get out of bed. My mom woke up briefly while putting on his pants and asked him what he was doing. I ducked down so she wouldn't see me. He told her he would return to the bathroom as she fell asleep.

I believe he was still drunk and wasn't thinking clearly as he slowly followed my instructions. I found out a long time before when I wanted something from someone. I could be very convincing.

I told him to hold on a second as he got to the front door. I needed to get something, and I'd be right back. As he waited, I went into my bedroom, got a loaded .38 pistol I had stolen a few years earlier, and stuck it in my belt. Before I went into my mom's bedroom to wake him, I grabbed a small hammer and a chisel from the toolbox in the garage and stuck them in my belt.

While driving to the store, I knew nothing was open except a little all-night quick-stop store near the middle of our small town. I told the big dummy to head in the opposite direction of the store. When we were away from the housing tracks and had come to a stop sign, I looked around to ensure there wasn't anybody around. I quickly reached over and threw the gear shift in the park. I then took out the .38 pistol and stuck it between his legs. I didn't hesitate as I shot him at point-blank range, right in his crotch. He immediately slumped over in pain and started screaming. I told him to shut up, or I would reshoot him, but the next one would be in the head.

I put the pistol to his head and told him to drive toward the woods. I told him where to go as we drove deep into the woods near the river.

When we got to where I wanted him, I had him stop. I told him to reach down with both hands and pull his shirt over his head. He was reluctant but still wrenching in pain, so he quickly did what I told him to do. He was begging me the entire time to take him to the hospital. After he pulled his shirt up over his head, I quickly took my shirt off and wrapped it around the gun. I didn't want any more blood splatter than I already had in the car, and I tried to muffle the sound of the gun. In a natural, calm, quiet voice, I said, "You shouldn't have pushed me around, you stupid asshole. Whose business do you think it is now?" I put the gun to his head and pulled the trigger. The blood and brain parts spattered on the driver's side window as he slumped toward the stirring wheel.

I quickly got out of the car and went to his side. I pushed him to the passenger side and jumped in the driver's spot. I drove his car further into a swampy area where I knew some deep quicksand near the river.

A few months earlier, I found this spot after killing the neighbor's dog because it wouldn't stop barking. It was beside the window where I slept, constantly barking all night. I had asked the neighbors several times to do something about the barking. I told them it kept me awake all night, and I needed to do something to stop it. They just ignored my request and refused to do anything about it. When they were sleeping, I killed it and took it to the river, where I dumped it in the quicksand. Now, that quicksand was coming in handy once again.

I dragged his body out of the car and over to the quicksand. I rolled him into it with all the evidence from his vehicle. I wiped off his blood from the window with my shirt, ripped out the part of the car's front seat where his blood had accumulated, and dumped it in the quicksand. I waited a few minutes to ensure everything had sunk and was out of sight. I chiseled the ID numbers off his car and then got back in, ran it into a big fat tree a few times in the front, and backed into it several times. I then knocked out all the windows with the hammer. I wanted it to look like a wrecked car. My heart was racing from all the excitement as I went about my plan. It was like I was someone else the entire time, but I was on a mission, and everything was falling into place.

I knew about an old wrecking yard not far away with many old beat-up cars, and it wasn't fenced in. That's where I planned to drop his car off. I drove the car in that direction, and when I got to within the last half mile, I cut all four tires, so it was just riding on bad tires and rims when I finally parked it. It was in bad shape, and I believed the junkyard owners might have thought one of their friends or someone they did business with had just left the beat-up car there for them.

I put the gun in one hand and the hammer and chisel in the other as I ran back to my house. I ensured no one saw me as I walked along the abandoned roads. When a car would come by, I ducked out of sight.

I was hyped up and very happy as I yelled and talked to myself as I returned home. I was huffing and puffing by the time I got there. It was just in time because it was starting to get daylight.

Later that morning, my mom woke up and wanted to know what had happened to the guy she had been with the night before. I said, "All I know is he got up early in the morning and didn't say a word to anyone as he crept out." My mom just shrugged her shoulders and said, "Oh well! You win a few and lose a few." She said that as she walked back into her room and closed the door.

Mom had ridden back from the bar with the guy. She had to get a ride from one of her friends back to where she had left her car.

While she was gone, I took a sledgehammer to the gun I had used to kill the guy and broke it up. I then took a hack saw and cut the barrel into three parts. Over the next few days, I dropped the gun pieces in the trash cans all over town.

That was my first experience killing someone, and I didn't think it was that big deal. It didn't seem much different than killing a cat or a dog. I remember being very pleased with myself because I never got caught for killing him.

My mom bar-hopped around the different towns for a few more years until she finally hooked up with some guy willing to put up with her and take care of my brothers. He also had a little money and was ready to spend it on her. He wasn't a bad guy to be around, and he kept my mom out of my hair, so I decided I wouldn't kill him. Even though, deep down inside, I still wanted my dad back. Somehow, I felt like this guy was just an obstacle that stood in the way. I also realized it would've been someone else if it weren't for him. I found ways to get out of the house as often as possible to keep from killing him.

A few years after my mom hooked up with him, I discovered that my dad had remarried a Paris, Texas, woman. I had just turned sixteen and gotten my driver's license. I found out where they lived and took a road trip to talk to him.

When I arrived at his house, his wife met me at the front door, and when I introduced myself, she said, "Your dad doesn't want to see you." I couldn't believe my ears, and I was in shock. I was so dumbfounded I didn't know what to say or do. I remember being devastated that I had traveled all that way, and she wouldn't, at least, let me talk to him. I was also angry that he didn't even have the guts to come to the door and tell me himself.

I made the trip and tried a couple more times again, and it was always the same answer from her. I didn't believe what she said, but my dad never contacted us after marrying her.

I never saw my dad alive again, and even after he died, his wife wouldn't tell me the location of his grave. I had a hard time with that type of behavior. I couldn't understand someone being so cruel and heartless to do something like that. During those trips to their house, I hated that woman and decided to kill her someday when I got a chance.

After my last trip to her house, I spent some time and studied the house and the town. I came up with a plan for how I was going to kill her. I waited about a month after I got home. I stole enough money to get a round-trip bus ticket and food to her home in Paris, Texas. I decided I wouldn't drive my car if someone saw me and could identify me as her killer.

I had already stolen another pistol and some bullets from a friend of mine's father. One day, when I was at my friend's house, the gun and ammo were lying on the kitchen table, and I stole them on the way out the door. His dad always told my friend that he believed I had taken it, but I always denied it when he asked me about it.

On the day I decided to journey to see my dad's wife, I stuck the pistol in my pants and wore my black hooded sweatshirt over my head with dark sunglasses. Before I left, I told my mom I would be gone for a few days to not worry about me. She asked me where I was going, and I just said I was going deer hunting with a few friends and would return in a few days.

I went to the bus depot and purchased the round-trip ticket under a fake name. The entire time I was on the bus to Texas, I just sat in the back corner and pretended to be asleep. I didn't want to talk to anyone or bring any attention to myself with what I had planned. All I could think about the entire way to her house was how angry I was that she wouldn't let me talk to my dad before he died. My hatred for her overwhelmed me the closer I got to her home. I had to whisper to myself to calm down, or I would ruin my plan. I kept running through my list repeatedly on exactly how I would kill her.

When I arrived in the middle of the afternoon, I thought it was perfect timing. I grabbed a hamburger and a coke at a local hamburger stand and then waited at a nearby park until it got dark.

I started walking toward her house once I felt it was dark enough. When I got there, the lights were on in her living room. It didn't look like anyone was visiting her because no cars were in the driveway. Studying her house for a while, I figured she must be alone.

I walked by her house a few blocks, then turned around and headed back. I checked the neighborhood to ensure no one was watching me as I slowly crept to her porch and looked in the windows. As I suspected, she was sitting on her couch watching television.

When I first saw her, rage welled in me, and I could feel the blood flowing down my face. I first thought I wanted to immediately burst into her house and shoot her right between the eyes. As hard as it was, I had to control my emotions because I had questions for her and wanted answers before I killed her.

I went around all the windows to ensure there wasn't anyone else in the house. Once I believed she was alone, I returned to the living room window and watched from the corner of the house for a few minutes to ensure no one in the neighborhood had seen me sneaking around. I made my move when it was safe and worked up enough nerve to follow my plan.

I went up to the front door, pulled out my pistol, and knocked on the door. At first, my dad's wife didn't answer the door, so I hit it again. Finally, after several minutes, she slowly opened the door and didn't recognize me as she started to say, can I help you? I quickly pushed my way inside. I told her not to scream, or I would put a bullet in her head.

That's when she knew who I was and asked me what I was doing there. I told her to close the curtains so none of the neighbors could see inside. I asked her if anyone else was in the house, and she slowly said no. She had two little dogs who were going crazy, barking and growling at me. I told her to put them in the bathroom, or I would kill them. She quickly picked them up as I followed her, carried them to the bathroom, and closed the door.

She said in an outraged voice, "What do you think you are doing here, Cody? Are you crazy?"

I told her to shut the fuck up and that I was the one that would be asking the questions.

I pulled out one of the chairs from under the kitchen table and used some ties from an apron she had lying on the counter in the kitchen. I ripped them off and tied her hands behind her back and the chair. I also tied her feet so she couldn't stand up and run. Now that I had her entirely where I wanted her, I began to ask her the questions I desperately needed her to answer. I asked her, "Why were you so heartless and mean to me when I made several attempts to see my dad before he died?

She said one of the things that I had suspected all along: "I decided that your dad didn't need to see you. According to what your father had told me, you had been nothing but trouble since you were born." Her words cut me like a knife, so I slapped her.

Then, in an angry voice, I asked, "Who gave you the right to keep me from my dad when all I wanted to do was talk to him? I wasn't trying to interfere with your marriage. I had a right to see and talk to him."

Her voice was quivering when she said she didn't feel I needed to be part of his life anymore. She said he had a good life with her and felt his kids from his previous marriage didn't need to be between them.

I told her, "I wanted to see my dad. I missed and loved him and wanted to know if he loved and missed me too."

That's when she said the hurtful things I didn't want to believe, "Your dad didn't love you, and he didn't want ever to see you again. He felt like you were just a pain in the neck to him and more trouble than you were worth." It was almost more than I could handle when she said those words. I felt like I was going to throw up. I almost shot her in the head, but I controlled my temper. If I hadn't had a plan, I would've killed her right then.

The tears rose in my eyes, and I said, "That's a lie. My dad would never have said those things about me."

That's when she continued her outburst, "Why do you think he wouldn't talk to you those times you came to see him?"

I had had enough of her and didn't want to hear any more from her, even if it was true. I still blamed her for not letting me in their house to see him. She could've been better and tried to explain how she felt. Even if I didn't understand her feelings, I would know why she felt the way she did. Now I was even angrier with her for saying what she was saying.

I was through talking to her. I ripped a piece of the apron apart, rolled it up in a ball, and stuffed it in her mouth. I told her, "You could've talked my dad into seeing me if you wanted to, but you didn't want me to be part of your little happy family. You just wanted him all to yourself. You didn't want him to have anything to do with me or my brothers. Now, look where it's gotten you. You're nothing but a lonely older woman sitting on your couch watching television alone with no one left in your life. I blame you for him feeling the way he did about me. He never felt that way before he met you. I feel like you kept us apart, and that's the way you wanted it." She just stared at me as her eyes filled with tears, and they began bugging out with fear.

She could tell that I was past listening to any reasoning. My emotions had finally taken control of me, and there was only one way this ordeal would end. At that point, I hit her in the head with the butt of the gun and knocked her unconscious.

I then went into the main bedroom and opened the closet, and some of my dad's clothes were still hanging. For a moment, as I stood there, all I could think about was how nice he looked in those clothes.

A thin leather brown belt was in one pair of his pants, so I grabbed it and returned to the kitchen. I thought a fitting end to my dad's wife's life would be using my dad's belt to kill her. I looked at her and slowly put the belt around her neck as I said, "You should've been nicer to me, bitch, and this would never have happened to you."

I could feel the anger and rage releasing me as I pulled the belt tighter and tighter around her neck. I choked her for several minutes until her limp body slumped over in the chair. I waited about five minutes, checked her wrist and neck for a pulse, and couldn't get one. That's when I knew she was dead.

I then went into her bedroom and started going through her drawers and throwing things on the floor to make it look like someone had broken in and robbed and killed her. I took all her jewelry and anything valuable to me to stick in my sweatshirt pockets. I went through her purse, took her cash, and threw everything on the floor. While rummaging through everything, I found a picture of my dad and stuck it in my pocket. After it looked like a robbery, I wiped everything clean, where I may have touched something. I also wiped the belt clean of any fingerprints.

After I had cleaned everything, I rechecked her pulse to ensure she was dead. After getting no response, I went to her back door, stepped outside, and broke it open from the outside. I left it open, returned to the front door, used a towel, turned off the lights, and opened the door as I slowly went outside. When I was sure no one watched the house, I left and headed back to the bus depot.

It took several hours for my mind and body to calm down, and I could finally sleep a few hours in the park. I was able to catch a bus early the following day. I did the same thing on my way back home as I had done there. I just sat in the corner of the back of the bus and pretended I was sleeping. Several times, I pulled out my dad's picture and cried softly. I was still hurting inside from my dad's wife's hurtful words about how he felt about me. What hurt me the most was that I would never know if they were genuine since he wasn't around to tell me any different. During a few stops along the way home, I got off to go to the bathroom. I disposed of the jewelry and the other things in the trash cans I had stolen from her house.

I was only sixteen, and I had already killed two people. The exciting thing about those killings was that I didn't feel remorse. I felt like both people I had killed deserved what they got.

Even though I had said it several times while I was growing up, it was during that time of my life that I promised myself that once I got married, it would be forever. I told myself that I would never put my kids through what I had gone through as a child. The woman I married in the future had to promise to live up to her marriage commitment to love and live with me forever. I had formed the idea that if my wife ever cheated on me or left me for another man, I would kill her and her lover.

***

Chapter 4 - Reflections of my childhood

When I was in prison, I had to be interviewed by a few phycologists and psychiatrists. They had to give the court mental evaluations of me to see if I was crazy. The psychiatrists wanted me to talk about my past and some things that had happened. They believed it led me to the point where I was in my mind. I began telling them about some of the best and worst times that were still vivid in my mind. During those interviews, I had forgotten about some exciting things as a child started rearing their ugly heads. Some reflections took me back to the dark part of my mind.

One such moment was when I was about five years old. I always tried my best not to get attached to any animals we owned when I was young. If we were to acquire a new dog, I wouldn't treat it very well because I knew we would leave it there and hope that someone else would take care of it as soon as we moved to a new location.

Several times when we moved, I remember looking out the back window of our car as we drove off and watching our dog follow until I couldn't see it anymore. That always made me cry to think that the dog wanted to be with us so much, yet we just abandoned it. After that happens a few times, you don't want to be close to an animal that loves you.

When dad finally left my mom, I felt like that's what he did to us when we were kids. He just abandoned us like he used to dump the dogs.

When I was six, we visited some relatives in Arkansas for a few days. My dad's brother decided they would kill one of the young goats they had been raising. He said it was what we were having for meat, and we stayed with them for the next few days. I had no idea what to expect, but my dad said, "Come on, Cody, let's go watch." I did what my dad wanted me to do in those early years, so I tagged along.

His brother cornered the young goat and flipped it on its back. He quickly tied its two front legs together and its two back legs together. He took this big, long hunting knife from a holster he was wearing and cut its throat while it was just sitting there looking around, wondering what was happening to it. I can still see its big, round, dark eyes looking at me. As soon as he cut its throat, the goat immediately let out a horrible scream that sent chills up and down my spine. I can still remember that its screams sounded like a woman in terrible pain. It scared me so bad that I wet my pants. I didn't let my dad know because I was too embarrassed to tell him what had happened. He probably knew but didn't let me know that he did.

They hung the dead goat up in the barn by its hind legs and started to skin it and gut it. At that point, I lost my appetite for goat meat. I told my mom and dad, "I'm not going to eat that goat."

After a few days of not eating anything, my dad said, "Cody, you can eat the goat meat or starve. It's your choice." When he told me that, I went into the bathroom and threw up for a few minutes. I was getting hungry, so after much disgust and total dissatisfaction, I ate the goat meat.

That wasn't my only experience with wetting my pants. I always wet my bed in the middle of the night until I was about eight or nine. My mom would get angry and sometimes whip me for it, but I didn't know how to stop it. Sometimes, I was afraid to go to sleep at night because, during the night, I would dream that I had to go to the bathroom badly. I always found a place to go in my dreams, and I would relieve myself. I thought it was a bathroom, but It turned out to be my bed, and I would wake up soaked in pee. It wasn't very comfortable, but I could do nothing to stop it. I would tell myself that I wasn't going to pee to bed when I first got in bed at night, but it never helped.

One day, I was spending the night at my cousin's house. I had to go to the bathroom in the middle of the night. I was half awake and half asleep, and I got up and started stumbling against the walls and looking for the bathroom door. I searched all over the room for the bathroom door but couldn't find it. By then, I had to go so bad I couldn't hold it any longer. I finally gave up looking and peed on the side of the wall in the middle of the room. That's when I finally woke up and realized what I had done. I was so embarrassed that I never told anyone about it, especially not my cousins. Yet, and much to my relief, one day, without rhyme or reason, the entire bedwetting just stopped.

I've always had an enormous dislike for cats. I hated them coming around me and rubbing against my legs, weaving in and around me, and wanting me to pet them. I felt like they were nothing more than just a pest instead of a pet. One day, when I was about eight years old, I talked a group of neighborhood kids into taking one of our neighbor's cats and pulling a trick on it. I got a dried-up corn cob and a bottle of hot rubbing cream. (That stuff burns like crazy when you put it on a new, fresh wound). I had one of the kids hold the cat's head; one held its two front legs, and another held its hind legs. I began to rub its butt with the corn cob. I rubbed it raw until it was bleeding and poured the cream on its butt. We then turned the cat free to watch and see what it would do. It let out a huge scream, made several circles trying to catch its tail, and then flew up into a twenty-foot tree straight to the top. You could tell it was in obvious pain because it was squirming around. It finally leaped from the top of the tree to the ground and took off running. We were all dying laughing, and I was so proud of myself for making all the kids laugh, all at the expense of that poor cat. It made me feel like I was the most important kid around. We never saw the cat again, but I didn't think it was a significant loss. I was glad it was gone.

When I was about ten, I had another encounter with a cat. Some stray cats kept coming to our house, wanting some food. My mom and dad always argued about them because she liked them coming around, and my dad didn't. She would feed them our scraps from the table. I got tired of hearing my mom and dad argue over the stupid cats, so one day, I went outside and found several pieces of wood, took some thick string, and made a bow and a few arrows. I decided I would get rid of those cats once and for all. I saw one hanging around the back door, so I started shooting at it. It took off running, and I started chasing it. It finally ran up into a tree for what it thought was safety. After several shots, one of my arrows found its target, and the cat came tumbling to the ground. I felt great joy and pride as I picked it up by the tail and said to it, "You won't be causing trouble around my house anymore, will you?" I had no feelings for the cat, so I was glad to get rid of it.

I killed a few more and chased the rest of them away with my bow and arrows. I foolishly believed what I had done would stop my mom and dad from fighting, but it didn't.

I was also a big prankster with my brothers and my cousins. Once, we were all out in the chicken barn collecting a few chickens to kill for dinner. When our cousins would visit, Mom would have me go out to the chicken pin, grab a few chickens, and then ring their necks. Watching them flop around even after their heads were gone was fun. On this occasion, I had some gum in my mouth, and I told my younger brothers and cousins that if they would take a handful of chicken feed, put it in their mouth, and chew it for a while, it would turn into chewing gum. I pretended to put chicken feed in my mouth and went through the chewing motion. Then, after a few minutes, I pulled out my chewing gum and showed it to them. I had all of them eating chicken feed by the time it was over. I kept telling them they didn't have enough and had to use more because it took a lot of chicken feed to make gum. (After trying for several minutes, they gave up because, "obviously," none made any gum).

One day, a neighbor friend of mine, who likes to cuss like crazy, played in a fort we had built up in an old tree about a mile from our house. It was down in this old, dried-up swamp area with lots of brush and overhanging trees. It was a great place to escape from home and pretend you were cowboys protecting the fort from the Indians. We each had BB guns, and we pretended to be the cowboys. It was a lot of fun to go and hang out there. I wouldn't say I liked staying around the home during those days because of my mom's and dad's issues.

I would take off early in the morning when I got up and stay gone all day. I would eat fruit from neighboring farms for lunch and wouldn't return home until dinner or just before dark.

One day, we heard a boy crying near us in the fort. My neighbor friend said, "What the hell is that?" We looked for the sound and found this boy about our age, just sitting in some bushes, and he was crying aloud. We cautiously approached him and asked him why he was crying. We also asked him his name. After he quit crying, he quietly said, Billy Joe Farris. We asked him what was wrong with him, but he wouldn't discuss it. The boy didn't live far from there but wouldn't say where. We invited him to come and play with us, and we told him he could become part of the cowboys if he would like. We told him he could go to the fort anytime he was sad or play alone.

Every time we saw him, he was sad, and after a while, he could trust us enough to tell us what was going on with him and why he was always so unhappy. He told us that his father had been molesting him for a few years, and he was embarrassed and ashamed to let anyone know. He said his father was molesting him, but he was molesting his sister as well. He said he hated his father and that he wanted to kill him. We all agreed that his father needed to die for doing that to him, but we didn't know what to do because we were just eleven-year-old kids and didn't have any guns or weapons.

My friend and I decided to talk to our parents about Billy and tell them what had happened to him. Much to our surprise, they wouldn't listen to us about it. They told us we should stay out of it because Billy might be lying about what his dad was doing and that it was none of our business.

My friend and I talked about it and decided we would call the police and tell them what Billy's dad was doing to Billy and his sister. We called the police and tried to talk to them, but because we were just kids, the police didn't believe us and wouldn't do anything about it. They must've thought we were just pranksters.

We decided to take the law into our own hands, so I devised a plan to write a letter to Billy Joe's dad and put it on his front door. We figured this would let him know the police knew what he was doing to his kids. We made two handwritten notes that said:

THE POLICE KNOW THAT YOU
ARE YOU MOLESTING YOUR KIDS?
IF YOU DON'T STOP, YOU ARE GOING TO JAIL.

We then snuck over to his house one night and put one on his front door and another in his mailbox. For some stupid reason, we thought this might scare him enough so that he would stop molesting his kids. It backfired on us.

We never saw Billy Joe Farris again after putting the letter on their door and in the mailbox. His father moved the family two days after we left the notes. We never found out where they moved to or what happened to him or his sister until later in his life.

I found out that Billy Joe Farris had killed two young people during a robbery when I was grown. After killing them, the police report said he ate the lunch they had just purchased from a fast-food restaurant. He received the death penalty and was later executed in California.

After visiting some cousins, I took my BB gun to their house. While my dad and mom were at home visiting my aunt and uncle, my younger brother, Michael, was riding an old bike he had found in the garage. He was going in big circles around the driveway. I decided to use him for target practice, so I fired a few shots at him. One of them bb's hit him in his left eye, and he hit the ground screaming. I thought he was faking until I ran over and looked him in the eye. When I saw it, I could tell I had messed it up. I was freaking out and scared to death. I knew my mom and dad would kill me when they discovered what I had done. In the hospital, I was slapped and hit by my mom.

Michael ended up losing that eye, and after we got home, my dad beat me with a belt for several minutes and again every day for about a week. My mom would slap me occasionally to let me know how unhappy she was with me. The lousy treatment they gave me for the next few weeks started making me feel less guilty about what I had done to my brother and the pain he had gone through.

I started getting angrier about the pain I had to endure. I began to welcome the beatings and the slaps because they helped ease the pain I felt for what I had done to Michael.

Not long after that incident, my parents got a divorce. That's when things started to change with me and my attitude. I was angry inside for losing my dad. I no longer had much of a conscience about the bad things I would do. I would do whatever I thought I could get away with without getting caught. I became very sly and calculative, gaining people's trust to steal things from them. When working for people, I would lie about how many hours I had worked. I felt alone and knew I had to take care of myself. No one else was going to.

I tried to go to school during those times, but I was always behind the other kids because we were constantly moving or never in the same place very long. That's the main reason I was not too fond of school. It wasn't that I was stupid. I had a hard time catching up with schoolwork. It seemed like some schools were ahead of what I had been learning. Some were behind what I had learned. It was always a challenge to go to a new school.

When I was about thirteen, I had a girl I liked who lived a few miles from my home in this worker's camp where many farm labor low-income housing people lived. Almost at her house, I saw some younger boys playing marbles. They didn't seem to be very happy, and a couple of them were crying. I noticed a boy about my size and age bending over and shooting the marbles out of a circle. The way we played marbles in those days is that you put your marbles in the center of a 3 to 4-foot circle. You would then flip a coin to see who goes first.

The first person would shoot at the marbles, trying to knock them out of the circle. It would help to keep all the marbles you shot out of the ring. Once your shooting marble left the ring, it would be the next guy's turn. The older kid had a coffee can that was almost full of marbles. He had won off the younger boys.

After watching him for a few minutes, I told him I didn't think it was fair to him to play those younger boys and take their marbles. He stood up, was a few inches taller and heavier than me, and told me to mind my own business, or he would beat the crap out of me. When he said that, I grabbed his coffee can full of marbles, threw them all over the ground, and told the boys to pick them up and keep them. That's when the older boy took a swing at me. I ducked and hit him twice in the face and told him to stop, or I was going to hurt him. Of course, he didn't take my advice, so I beat him up with my fists. I blacked both of his eyes and busted his lip and nose. He was bleeding all over his face when I told the stupid bully that if he did that to the boys again, I would come back. I felt like he should've listened to me and wouldn't have gotten beaten up.

When I was almost seventeen, I lived with my cousins in California to finish my last two high school years. No one knew it, but I had already killed two people then. One of my cousins was my age, and another was two years younger. The first year was great fun being with them and going to school. It was just like having my brothers, but closer to my age. Something about me that always bothered them was constantly getting into fistfights. I even got into fights with some of their best friends. I couldn't help it. I had a chip on my shoulders. I had been through hell at that point, and no one knew or understood. They couldn't understand why I was so willing to fight. I didn't even understand it myself. They said I had a mean, angry look on my face when I would confront someone. They said it was a little scary. I would look a little mean when I got mad, but it was more about the sadness I felt inside than anything.

On the other hand, I always had a very soft-sounding or quiet spoken voice, and people said it was hard to hear me talk sometimes. My idol during those years was the actor James Dean. I tried hard to emulate the way he spoke and dressed in movies.

No matter how hard I tried, I always felt like a fish out of water at my cousin's school. DURING THOSE DAYS, I only liked wearing a black body-fit T-shirt, Levi's, and cowboy boots. Most guys my age were wearing matching clothes. Many girls liked me because of that "tough guy" persona, but for the most part, I didn't fit into the clean-cut high school kid mold. I also liked wearing my dark brown hair a little longer than average and combed straight back.

I knew my time living with my cousins would be short-lived, but we had much fun while it lasted. My cousins didn't share the same "it doesn't matter attitude" type that I possessed.

I always tried to use the system to get what I wanted. If I couldn't get it by asking for it, I would try taking it by force or finding a way to steal it. I never had to pay for gas for my car; I just stole it from the farmers' tanks that lived in the country. They usually had four or five-hundred-gallon gas tanks behind their houses for their tractors and vehicles. The only thing keeping me out was a little padlock, which was easy to break. I would canvas their home, wait for them to go somewhere, and then steal what I needed. The key to not getting caught was never trying to steal from the same farm twice.

I went to "Shotgun Effie's house" to steal gas one night. Her place was out east of town. I don't know her real name, but everyone around town called her "Shotgun Effie" because she had shot at a few people with her shotgun for trying to steal fruit from her trees. I watched her house for a few hours and couldn't see anything happening in or around it. She lived in a big old two-story house that looked about 100 years old. It was brown and shabby, and I don't think it had been painted for about that long as well. I drove slowly into her driveway and went to the back, where her gas tanks stood. I got out of the car like

I owned the place and broke the lock on the gas tank. Everything was fine as I took the gas that I needed.

When I finished with the gas, I saw some ripe peaches on one of her trees. They looked so inviting that I decided to go to the trees and steal one or two of them. As soon as I picked some peaches from the tree, I heard the screen door slap the house as it shut behind this little, humped-over, wrinkled, gray-haired woman. I looked at her, and she had a shotgun in her hands. I immediately started running for my car. I heard her saying in a high-pitched voice, "Stay away from my peaches," as she fired the shotgun at me. She might have been old, but she had a pretty good aim. I felt this tremendous pain in my back, like I had just been stung by a hundred honeybees simultaneously. I ran, got in my car, and took off. I felt safe as soon as I got far away from her place.

I was squirming around as I pulled over to see how badly I was wounded. I wanted to see how much blood I had on my shirt. I pulled off my shirt, and much to my surprise, I didn't have much blood coming from what I was sure were pellet wounds in my back. My back was still stinging, and I was wrenching in pain when I realized she had shot me in the back with shells loaded with rock salt instead of pellets. Although it burned for several hours, I was lucky she used rock salt, or I might've been dead. That's one place I made sure I never went back there again.

One night, my cousins and I got in trouble with the police for beating on a wooden box with our fists. It covered an outdoor jukebox at the local hamburger joint in town. We hit the boards to see who could break one of them with our fists. I think each one of us broke at least one. It was about 2:00 when the police woke my aunt and uncle and asked them to get us out of bed to take us down to the police station. We were all scared we would go to jail for a few days. My aunt and uncle talked to the police, and they had to pay a few hundred dollars for the broken boards to keep us out of the juvenile hall. That was the last straw with them, and they said I had to go.

That was during my senior year of high school, and I had worn out my welcome with my Aunt and Uncle, and it was time to move back home with my mom and brothers. It seemed like no matter what I did, I never fit in with my family or anyone else. I felt like a lost soul like I didn't belong anywhere. I didn't feel like anyone cared if I lived or died at that point in life. I wouldn't say I liked living with my mom anymore, but I had no choice. I didn't have any place else to go.

***

Chapter 5 - My cousin Jodie

My mom moved into a little shack of a house not too far from my grandparent's home in California. That's where I went to live for a while. I think I was around seventeen and a half years old. That's when I met my cousin, Jodie. She was 15 at the time. Her parents had sent her to live with our grandparents for two months during the summer. She was beautiful, and I thought she probably was among the most beautiful girls I'd ever seen. She was about 5'6" with long black hair down past her shoulders and soft blue eyes. She had a body that you would only see in Playboy magazines. As soon as we met each other, we started doing everything together. No matter where I went, she wanted to go with me. I loved all the attention she was giving me. It was the first time in my life that someone liked me for who I was.

After a few weeks of being together, I took her to my old swimming hole in one of the irrigation canals, about two miles from our house. I had learned to swim just a few years earlier when my cousins took me to a canal near their home. I told them that I didn't know how to swim. (That wasn't entirely true; I couldn't float on the top of the water). I learned to hold my breath and swim under the water for about a minute. They thought they were funny and grabbed me, wrestled me down to the dark, murky water of the nearby canal, and threw me in. Before I went under, I took a deep breath, swam to the bottom, and kept floating about fifty yards downstream. I came up for air, found some overhanging weeds, and hid in them with just my head above water.

After throwing me in the water, my cousins didn't see me and thought I had drowned. They started running up and down the canal banks, looking for my body. I was sitting in the water and laughing at them while peering through the weeds the entire time. I let them suffer for throwing me in the water when they thought I couldn't swim. They were starting to panic after about fifteen minutes, and I could tell they were getting ready to get help to search for me. That's when I swam upstream until I returned to where they threw me in and crawled out. The big joke ended up being on them and not me. After that, they taught me how to do the breaststroke and the freestyle, and it didn't take me very long to learn.

Jodie and I had to walk down dirt paths and roads to get to my favorite swimming hole. It was very secluded, and we would swim nude most of the time. She didn't seem to mind removing all her clothes before me. We would lay out on the edge of the canal bank on the towels we had brought and soak up the sun. She looked terrific when that hot afternoon sun would sparkle off her wet body. Sometimes, she would turn a certain way, and I could see the silhouette of her body just glowing. I could look at her for hours, and she drove me crazy. She had beautiful curves and lovely, complete, and firm breasts.

We talked about everything that young people talk about, and it was easy for us to talk. Sometimes, I would hitch a ride into town from neighbors to hang out, and she would go with me. She was a blast to be with, and I loved every minute of her attention.

Soon, our attraction toward each other became more than just cousins. We found ourselves flirting and teasing more and more with each other. We started entering the bedroom and making out when no one else was around. She had great full lips and didn't mind me putting my hands wherever I wanted to on her body. I loved touching her and kissing her. The sex with her was a little awkward because it was her first time, but then it got terrific after a few more times of being together. We were like two new lovers that couldn't get enough of each other. I knew she was my cousin, but I couldn't help myself. I couldn't resist her. I don't know how she kept from getting pregnant, but she did. Lucky for us because we would probably have had a creepy-looking kid. I think what we had for each other was "puppy love" during those two months. We both knew it was wrong and wouldn't last, but it was so much fun while it lasted.

Our grandparents didn't know what was happening and didn't suspect anything between us because we were cousins. They thought we just liked hanging out with each other. They didn't bother us, even when they would come in and see us sleeping in the same bed.

Looking back, it was probably good that she went back home after her two months were up. There's no telling what would've happened if we had gotten caught by my mom or her parents. We vowed to each other that we would never get together again after that summer, but it was a time I would never forget.

After she left and returned home, I remember feeling all too familiar, empty, and sad once again.

***

Chapter 6 - Hanging out with Buddy

My mom's youngest brother's name was Harlan, but everyone called him Buddy. He was only about six years older than me, and I formed a huge attachment to him when I was young. I looked up to him and idolized him. I always wanted to be around him or hang out with him. That was not good for me because he always got into fights or some other kind of trouble as he got older. He would spend several stints in jail.

I started hanging out with Buddy right after Jackie left and returned home. At that time, he wasn't married but had four kids. We both could use the company, so we started doing many things together. He took me under his wing and said he wanted to teach me everything I needed to know about life. He didn't realize that I had already been to hell and back, living with his sister, my mom. We became more like brothers than anything else during that time. We spent almost all our time with each other.

He was about 5'10" and attractive, stocky, and well-built. He had a tremendous country-western singing voice. I always thought he was good enough to sing with the best country singers like Merle Haggard and Buck Owens, but he lacked the confidence to be a star. He taught me how to play the guitar and sing, but I didn't have the voice or the talent he had.

At one point, we decided to take a trip to Oklahoma. He and I both wanted to go, but we had little money. He said, "Don't worry about the money; we'll get some girls to give us money along the way." I thought he was crazy and didn't believe him, but he was right. We would stop in some tiny country and western bar, go in, and sit down at the bar, and soon, we would have girls coming over to talk to us.

We would dance to a few songs with them and tell them how beautiful they were. It wasn't long before the girls sat with us and bought us drinks. If we didn't go home with them, we would have them get a hotel room. We would get some liquor and then party with them and usually have sex with them for the rest of the night. We would then get up early, shower, and get ready to go to our next place. Sometimes, we would go through the girls' purses while they were in the bathroom or take a shower before we left. We would take some of their cash, sneak out, and go there alone.

Sometimes, we would get into huge fistfights with some old country boys in the bars who thought we were trying to pick up their girlfriends. Most of the time, they were right, but we were both brutal and didn't mind getting into a fistfight now and then. There weren't too many guys that could whip us as a team.

Sometimes, Buddy would talk the owner or manager of the bar into letting him play the guitar and sing for a few hours to get extra money or free drinks. He always put on a great show and made everyone in the bar want more. Usually, while he was singing, I would have some wild little country girl all over me, or I would have her in the car's back seat.

Every time we got low on cash, we'd stop at one of those little bars and hook up with some girls. We always had enough money for gas and food to contact us at our next stop. It was so easy that Buddy never cared about the girl's appearance. He didn't care if they were ugly or pretty. They were all the same to him. He always said, "The ugly ones are the ones that'll give you everything they have if you are nice to them or have sex with them." He always had his share of the pretty girls, but he never could get much money out of them.

When we got to our relatives in Oklahoma, they would get everyone together for a big family gathering, and the family members would bring food and drinks. Buddy and I played music and sang. Everyone seemed like they were happy to see us. We stayed about a week, and relatives gave us money to help us return to California when we were ready. We stopped a few more times on the way back and had fun with some of those country girls as before, but at different bars.

Buddy and I made several trips back and forth from California to Oklahoma for about three to four years. It was the same the first few times, and our focus started to change.

On our way back to Oklahoma, I remember one time we went into a car dealership and talked them into letting us have a new car with no money down! Contracts only took a handshake or a man's word or promise. We used fake names to buy the car and told them we would be the next day to make the down payment. They let us drive off with it, and we never paid a dime. We had it for about a week and eventually abandoned it somewhere in the country, in one of the states we passed through. As soon as we got rid of one, we would get another to contact us where we needed to be.

Sometimes, we did those things to see if we could get away with it more than anything else. We could talk people into giving us just about whatever we needed with a bit of convincing and a slick word.

Then things changed, and if we couldn't get money from the girls or someone else, we would canvas a store to see if the clerk was alone. If they were alone, we would rob it, taking what we needed. Or, if we saw a person dressed nice, who looked like he had money on him, and was walking along the street alone, we would beat him up and take his money. I noticed our trips and activities were becoming increasingly violent. When you're living that type of lifestyle, it doesn't take too long before you're going to get caught.

A few years later, we rolled a guy to get his money, and that's when Buddy's luck ended. He was spotted and identified by the police as the person who did the robbing. Buddy wouldn't tell the cops that I was with him, so he took the full rap for the robbery. He spent a few years in prison in California for that robbery. He had taken the blame for something that we both had done, but early on, we had agreed that if one of us ever got caught and the other didn't, the one that got seen would take the entire blame for the job.

We both knew that eventually, one of us or both would get caught and have to pay the consequences for our actions. We just weren't sure which one of us it would be.

During our last trip together and before he went to prison for a second time, he told me a big secret he had carried with him for several years. He said that when he and his wife split up for the last time, she started going to the bars and picking up guys to go home with before their divorce was final. Even though they weren't living together, he said it hurt him to see her with someone else. He said he caught her with a guy in a bar parking lot one night. He said he severely beat the guy and then beat her until he was sure she was dead. He said he just left her there and never went back. He always believed the cops would be looking for him and eventually find him and throw him in jail for killing her. He said it was odd that he never heard a word from anyone, whether she was dead or alive.

He said that the incident did something to him inside and changed his life. I tried to sympathize with him when I said, "If you were still married to her, then maybe she deserved what she got." I wouldn't say anything to him differently because that's exactly how I believed things should be.

While he was in prison the second time, I met a girl from the small valley town in California where my grandparents lived. I ended up having a couple of boys with her. It was sad, but I wasn't really in love with her. I tried hard to make it work with her; we lived together for three to four years. I worked odd jobs here and there but wasn't happy.

Finally, one day, I just had enough of living a lie and left. The hardest thing about splitting with her was giving up my two boys because I didn't want to be like my dad. Unfortunately, the ties to my sons would keep me forever attached to California. It was always hard for me because it was a tug-of-war with my heart between my boys and my one true love, Oklahoma. That's the place I always wanted to be. I loved that you could hunt deer or wild pigs and go fishing whenever possible. It was like paradise to me.

After Buddy escaped prison, we decided to make a few more trips back and forth from California to Oklahoma. Every trip we made became more violent than the last. On my previous trip with him, we robbed people at gunpoint or beat them up and took whatever money they had on them. We figured we needed it more than they did.

Fearing that we may spend the rest of our lives in prison, we decided we would lay low for a while once we returned to California for the last time. That was when we stopped hanging out together as often.

***

Chapter 7 - Meeting Cori

Soon after I quit hanging out with Buddy, I met the woman I fell in love with, Corinne Compton, California. She was 23 years old and about seven years younger than me. She had a son named Jason from a previous marriage and couldn't have anymore. She was in a bitter custody battle with her ex-husband, who was in law enforcement. Her son was four years old and needed his mom and a dad. I was also at the point where I was ready to settle down.

From the first moment I saw her, I knew I had to make her my wife. I had never met anyone like her before, and it didn't take long before I fell deeply in love with her. She had olive-colored skin, long, dark, wavy brown hair, and emerald green eyes. I thought she was beautiful. She was very friendly and easy to talk to, and the best part for me was that she fell in love with me. I finally discovered what I had missed with all the other women I had been with. I felt like she was the perfect woman for me, and our bodies seemed to fit like a glove when we made love. We loved each other so much, which made that part of our lives even better. Having sex with her meant "making" love for me. That was the one thing in our relationship I thought neither of us would ever tire.

After all the years together, I knew I never got tired of being with her. I also never got tired of having sex with her. Sometimes late at night, I still fanaticize about her whispering, "I love you, Cody Dean Walker." She was MY woman, my possession. I felt like "I OWNED HER BODY AND SOUL." No man could ever have her or ever touch her again.

We both had a lot in common, and I guess that's what drew us together in the first place. We told each other that it would be for life once we committed. There would never be any backing out of the relationship or divorce for either of us. I told her, "Just don't ever, ever, ever cheat on me because I made a promise to myself when I was young that if my wife ever cheated on me, I would kill her." She knew that I was serious about cheating and in my beliefs and threats. Even so, she still wanted to be with me. She used to tease me about being so jealous.

I still hear those words as she said, "You don't have anything to worry about, Cody Dean Walker. I would never cheat on you."

We were living the perfect young married lover's life, but something was still missing for her and me. She was missing her son terribly and wanted to be with him all the time but couldn't because she had to share his custody with her ex-husband. I was doing farm labor work during those times, which wasn't enough for me. I wanted more out of my life for Cori, Jason, and myself.

Oklahoma seemed to be calling me back home. If I stayed in California, I'd never be the person I wanted to be. At the same time, we constantly fought with her ex-husband over her son. That's when we devised a plan and decided she would kidnap her son, and the three of us would go somewhere in Oklahoma and never let him know where we were. After careful planning, she had Jason on the weekend; we decided to take him and never look back.

On the way to Oklahoma, I told Cori we should find a place in Arkansas because no one would look for us there. They would be looking for us in Oklahoma. She agreed so that's where we went. We found a little town called Broken Arrow, just over from the Oklahoma line in South/West Arkansas, and decided to settle there.

We were not far from Queensland, which was the county seat. I didn't know it then, but it was considered one of Arkansas's best fishing and hunting areas. It was in the Ouachita Mountains, which consisted of a few million acres of wooded mountains that run east and west. Ouachita is the Indian name for "good hunting grounds." Queensland had a large lake called DeQueen Lake and a large river.

Highway 70, east and west, and Highway 71, heading north and south, were not too far out of Queensland. They were the two major roads leading in and out of the area. Broken Arrow was so small that there was only a post office, a small bank, and a country store. There was also an old hotel and a cafe. The town and all the people in and around it totaled no more than 500 people.

Eight small towns were within a ten-mile radius of the city, but we were about 45 miles from Texarkana's. This little scenic town was perfect for us. It had rolling hills and many trees, and everyone seemed to keep to themselves, which was a bonus for us. Five lakes were within driving distance and lots of small creeks and rivers. I soon found this would be a great place to hunt and fish. It was precisely what we sought, with all the mountains, rivers, and lakes. The summer temperature wasn't much above the '90s, but the humidity was high. The winters were a little chilly at 30 to 40 degrees from late December to February, but that didn't seem bad.

We rented a little three-bedroom house in town and settled in. We figured that her ex could never find us there. Cori had faith and believed in me. Being together was all that mattered to us at that time.

Because of my ability to manipulate people, most felt like I was just an honest, reasonable, hard-working guy. It didn't take long, and I met the Mayor of Queensland. I lied to him and told him that I had been in Law enforcement when I lived in California. (Even though it was a lie, he didn't know it and never checked on me). He was so impressed with me he soon called me to say they needed a deputy Sherriff in Queensland. Lucky for me, he used his influence to get me the job. I was always grateful to him for helping me out.

I tried hard to be that good old family man and give up my hidden, unlawful ways.

We found out from family members in California that there was an arrest warrant for Cori for kidnapping her son. From then on, we had to lay low because we didn't want to lose her son, and she didn't want to go to prison for kidnapping. We knew she would never be able to set foot in California again because of that.

I spent all my time learning my job with Cori and Jason for the next few years. I would take Jason with me everywhere I went. I taught him how to fish, ride a bike, and hunt deer. I taught him how to shoot a rifle and pistol when he was about five. I liked spending time with him. He was a terrific kid, and we couldn't have been any closer than if he had been my flesh and blood.

The three of us would spend our weekends having barbeques and enjoying each other's company. Cori and I were getting along incredibly, delighted, and in love. We spent much time at night when I wasn't busy, just cuddling on the couch and watching television together. Those were great times and the ones I remember and loved the most.

My job as a Deputy Sheriff was mainly quiet, but I had to drive daily to cover all the little towns in my county. Most of my arrests were for poaching, growing pot, speeding, or domestic disturbance.

Whenever I caught someone with weed, I confiscated it and kept some for myself. Then, I let the person go free. I didn't figure that was a big thing because I enjoyed smoking pot from time to time myself. It was an easy job, and I liked it. After a few years on the job, they promoted me to county Sherriff. I then had complete control to do whatever I wanted.

***

Chapter 8 - Encounter in Albuquerque

A few years passed, and I missed my two sons, still living in California with their mother. I didn't want them to think I had abandoned them the way my dad did me. After discussing it with Cori, I decided to visit California for a few days and see them. I took one of the weeks of paid vacation I earned from work and left the following Friday morning.

I left before the sun came up, around 4:00 am, when I left. If you weren't familiar with the roads in that area, you would usually head up highway 71 to Fort Smith and then take highway 40 straight through to California. Since I knew the streets well, I took a shortcut, went up through McAlester, Oklahoma, and then caught highway 40 heading west. That saved me some time. I figured I could make it to Albuquerque, New Mexico, by nine or ten that evening, then stop and take a quick nap in my car before going any further.

After driving for about sixteen hours, I finally started looking for a place to take a catnap. I found a country bar with a big, dark parking lot and crashed there for a few hours before some drunken people woke me up with laughter and loud voices. I had to go to the bathroom, so I went to the bar. A lot was going on, and many people were in the bar. They had a small western band playing, and people were dancing and having a good time. It was my kind of place; it was dark and had a long bar against one wall. I loved country music and figured I would enjoy it for a few minutes.

I grew up listening to country music, and I'd been in bars like this for as long as I could remember. I was hunting for my mom in the bars. I was not too fond of bars when I was a kid, but now that I was older, I liked them and the people who hung out in them. I loved the homegrown country girls that were always hanging around them. They were easy to talk to and sometimes easy to pick up and take home.

After going to the bathroom, I found an empty stool at the bar and ordered a beer. I wasn't planning to stay too long, but maybe I would have a few beers, listen to the music, and then head out. A pretty little blond caught my eye as I looked at the dance floor. Her hair was long, and she had a nice, well-built body. She wore a short skirt, boots, and a tight top showing her lovely full breasts. I felt like she was trying to show off that body. She looked like she was between 25 to 30 years old and a little drunk. She looked sexy while she was dancing by herself on the dance floor. I must have caught her eye because she kept smiling at me.

I smiled back a few times and returned to my drink. I knew I didn't have time for this and didn't want to get involved with her. The next thing I knew, she was standing against me with her body pressing against my leg. She slurred as she said, "I like you, cowboy. What's your name?" I told her and then took a drink from my beer bottle. I felt flattered that she liked me, but that was it. It was hard to ignore that she was so sexy, and her body did feel good against mine.

While I was enjoying our little talk, some big guy slapped me on the back and said," Hey, that's my wife; you're flirting with you, SON OF A BITCH!!" He didn't realize it, but those words were something you didn't call a person. I was six feet tall and weighed about 190 pounds, but this guy was slightly more significant than me. I wasn't scared of him; I didn't want my boys to see me covered in bruises and cuts when I arrived in California from a bar fight. I stood calmly and said, "Hey, man, I'm not looking for trouble. I'm sorry if I did something to offend you."

The blond quickly scurried away when that happened. At first, I thought that was it, and then the confrontation ended. The guy tried to get me to fight him, but it didn't work. I had seen this mouthy type of guy many times before and had whipped a few of them just for being so stupid. I sat down to finish my beer, and he returned grumbling obscenities.

The bartender approached me and said, "Pay no attention to him; he comes in here a lot with his wife, and he's just a big loudmouth, troublemaker."

While sitting there, the words S.O.B. he'd called me weren't sitting well with me. They kept repeatedly replaying in my head and eating at me. Maybe unconsciously, I did feel like my mom was a bitch, and those words, son of a bitch, stung like one of those switches across my back. It hurt me somewhere very deep inside to feel that way about her. Still, I wasn't going to let someone else call my mom a bitch.

Sitting at the bar, I devised a plan and decided to do something to get back at this big loudmouth. I couldn't let him think he could get away with saying something like that to me. I waited for the right moment as his wife made her way near me again; I reached over, gently grabbed her by the hand, and pulled her close. I whispered in her ear, "Meet me alone outside in fifteen minutes, and I'll show you how a real cowboy can give you a good time." I kissed her on the neck, stood up, threw money on the bar for my drink, thanked the bartender, and left.

I didn't know if she would meet me outside, but it was worth a try. Sure enough, after about fifteen minutes, she came running out alone. I waved for her, and she came running over to meet me. We immediately started kissing each other. I walked her over to my car and passionately kissed her on the neck. Even though she was a little drunk, she was sweet. I lifted her skirt, ran my hand down inside her panties, and rubbed between her legs as I kissed her. She gasped as I started rubbing her soft spots and firm body. She was already wet from dancing, but I didn't mind that. She was breathing fast as she whispered in my ear, "You better hurry. We don't have much time."

I then turned her around, leaned her forward against a car, pulled her skirt and panties down, and then unzipped my pants and pulled them down. I grabbed a handful of her blond hair and hummed her hard. She had an excellent firm and tight body, and it felt good. The more I thought about her husband and what he had said to me, the harder I humped her. She seemed to like it but was scared her husband would catch us as she kept looking back at the bar. She was a good sport and waited for me to finish and then quickly pulled up her panties and skirt down.

I didn't think she got much out of it, but maybe it was just the excitement of someone new for her. Sometimes, with sex, that's all you need. As she left, she said, "Thanks, cowboy, I liked that," kissed me and ran back into the bar. Just like that, half my plan was now complete.

I got into my car, drove it about two blocks from the bar, and parked in a dark area. I grabbed a tire iron out of my trunk and headed back to the bar to finish the second half of my plan. I decided I would hide in some bushes until they came out. I didn't have to wait too long before they came stumbling out, alone and pretty drunk. I followed them to their car, ensuring no one else was around to see me.

Just as he started to get into his car, I hit him in the head with the tire iron, and he went down. When I did that, his wife started screaming toward the bar. I didn't hit him hard enough to kill him because I wanted him to hear what I had to say to him, and I wanted him to think about it once I was gone. I then hit him with a breaking blow to his right kneecap and one to his left knee cap. I could hear the crunching sound as each one shattered. I knew it would be a while before this jerk could walk again, and that's what I wanted.

As he was lying there, squirming, screaming, and crying in pain, I leaned down and said, "You shouldn't have called me a SON OF A BITCH. You don't call someone's mother a bitch unless you know her." I then got in his face and said, "Thanks for letting me fuck your wife while you were in the bar getting drunk, your big stupid idiot. She was great, and I loved having sex with her. You should take better care of your woman, dumbass. She's a real catch, but it's too bad you don't appreciate her."

I just wanted to let my words about his wife sink in and haunt him like what he said about my mom. It only took me a few minutes to rough the guy up, but I knew some guys from the bar or the police would be there soon.

I took off running to my car as fast as I could go. I threw the tire iron in the back of the trunk and was back on the main road heading to California. I was out of sight before anyone realized what had just happened.

The adrenaline rush kept me going, and I was wide awake for the rest of the drive to California. I couldn't help, but the more I thought about the incident, the more I kept laughing aloud about the whole ordeal. I thought *the big, tough guy got what he deserved, and I got to make love to his wife.* I kept thinking about what a big dumbass he was.

I did have to make a few pit stops along the way, but I made it to California the next day. I was glad to see my boys. They had grown so much that I hardly recognized them. We spent three good days together, and I enjoyed being with them.

On my last day there, I told my boys I couldn't see them for a few years, and then I headed back to Broken Arrow. I had to be at work the following Monday. I left Friday morning and was back in Broken Arrow by Sunday morning. I didn't sleep much on the way home. I couldn't wait to see Cori because I missed her.

***

Chapter 9 – Incident with the homeless guy

When I got home, I returned to a pleasant working routine, coming home and being with my family. We spent our weekends fishing and having BBQs. Occasionally, I would go out hunting and take Jason with me, and most of the time, I would get a deer or a wild pig to have enough meat for the freezer. We always had the freezer full of games and never had to buy any unless we wanted chicken or beef.

One day, we heard that our elderly neighbor, who lived down the road, had died, and her son was selling the property. He was willing to carry the mortgage note on the property with little money as a down payment. The price and terms were right for us. We needed it because we didn't have to record any deeds.

The property was a twenty-acre piece of fenced-in property. It was in the country and about three miles from town. It had a three-bedroom older house at the end of a winding dirt road, about a quarter-mile off the main road. The nearest neighbor was over a half-mile away. It was perfect for us. It gave us the privacy and freedom we'd been looking for since we arrived in Broken Arrow. I began repairing the place and mending fences to have a few cattle and raise our chickens for meat and eggs. We were so excited to have this place and loved it.

I finally felt like I had a permanent home for the first time and didn't have to move away anymore. I just had to ensure Cori was happy and that she never got caught for her son's kidnapping.

During my time on the job, I let many people get away with things that they might typically have had to spend some time doing behind bars. I felt that was okay because I gained a reputation around the county for being tough but fair.

Being the Sherriff, I had to work the entire county, not just my little town, so I ensured I spent time in all the other little towns.

Sometimes, things would get interesting, especially when I would catch a young married girl for speeding. They almost always wanted me to let them out of the ticket, so they would offer to "work something out with me." Most of the time, I would warn them and send them on their way unless it was the second or third time I had caught them doing the same thing. Occasionally, if she offered and attracted her, I would have her follow me to a turn out in the woods. I would have some quick sex with her if she were married and let her out of the ticket.

I always told the girls that if anyone found out about what we had done, I would come looking for her and tell her husband that sex was her idea. I knew that would be enough to keep me safe. Those sex acts were never like my intimate relationship with Cori; I just considered them pure sex and different from making love. That was the way I justified it in my mind.

Sometimes, I would get a big guy who had too much to drink, and he would be driving while drunk. If he reminded me of one of my mom's old boyfriends or he was belligerent, I would pull him out of the car and rough him up a little. If he gave me trouble, I would just beat him and say that he resisted arrest, and then I'd throw him in jail for a day or two. I always ensured no witnesses were around to see what I had done.

I would sometimes catch guys killing a deer out of season, and I'd make a deal with them to share some of their meat with me, and then nobody had to know they were breaking the law. Most of my working days were routine and boring because not much happened.

Things went on like that for a few more years, and then I started getting the urge to see my boys again. They were almost 10 and 11 years old, so I talked to Cori and decided to use another week of paid vacation time and take a California trip. This time, I told myself I wouldn't stop in Albuquerque, New Mexico. I decided to drive to Gallup, New Mexico, before stopping to rest.

I left again early in the morning and arrived at Gallop about 19 hours later. It was around midnight, and I needed just a little sleep before I kept driving. It would then be okay to go to California the rest of the way. I found a nice, quiet place near a city park to nap. It was dark there, and I thought I would be safe and away from everything. I had guns I carried with me everywhere I went for protection. I even had a few illegal ones that I had taken from a few guys that didn't have permits. I also brought a baseball bat to the passenger seat.

After a few hours of sleep, I heard a tapping on my window. I was still half asleep when I woke up and found a dingy, dirty-looking guy asking me if he could get a ride from me. At first, it startled me, and I said, "No, I don't want anyone riding with me." I just wanted to be left alone. I figured he would get in my way or try to rob me. I had some cash, and I couldn't afford to lose it.

When I said he couldn't have a ride, he soon became very agitated and violent and hit my window with his fist. Luckily for me, it didn't break. He then started kicking my car and shouting that he wanted a ride. I looked around to see if anyone else in the park or nearby might have watched what he was doing. I didn't see anyone, so I grabbed my baseball bat and jumped out of the car. When I did that, the guy saw the bat in my hand and pulled out a long hunting knife. He then said he wanted my money and would cut my throat if I didn't give it to him. When he said that, I hit him with the bat in the right shin just below the knee, and he went down, moaning. Once he was on the ground, I got in his face and asked why he didn't leave me alone. I wasn't looking for an answer. I was now angry. I very calmly said, "Really, are you that stupid? You would've been much better off if you had just walked by and left me alone." He said he was sorry when I hit him with two killing blows, one to the side of his head right above his right ear, and he stiffened up. Then I hit him with another one right across the bridge of the nose while he was lying on his back, jerking around. I crushed his nose into his skull because I could hear the crunching sound as the hardwood met his nose and face. That was it; just like that, it was over almost as quickly as it had begun.

I left him with his knife still in his hand, took my bat, and put it back in the car. I ensured there were no witnesses when I quickly left that place. As I left, I said, *what a stupid idiot. He should have left me alone. He deserved what he got.*

This time, I didn't have the same thrill I had on my last trip through New Mexico. The drive drained me emotionally, and the ordeal with the homeless guy. The rest of the trip to California was tiring and uneventful, as I made it there the next day to see my sons.

We were all delighted to see each other, and again, I couldn't believe how much they had grown. As the boys got a little older, I went back to see them several times, but I didn't run into any trouble coming or going on those trips. Cori and Jason were always happy to see me when I returned home. I was always excited to return home and settle into my routine with my family and work.

***

Chapter 10 - The child molester

One of the things that I was adamantly against was child molesters. I knew a few kids like Billy Joe Farris growing up molested for years, and somehow his scum bag father had gotten away with it. Now that I was a Sherriff, I wouldn't let someone in my county get away with doing that to a defenseless and helpless child.

One day, I stopped an old, beat-up Ford car because of a busted taillight. It had a car full of kids and a female passenger. The driver wasn't friendly when I asked him for his license and registration. I could tell he lived away from town and deep in the woods. I told him I wouldn't give him a ticket; I just wanted him to fix his taillight. He had four kids in the back seat, and I didn't want someone running into the back of them and hurting the kids.

The more I tried to talk to the guy, the more agitated he became. His attitude started angering me, so I asked him to leave the car. As he got out of the car, he became angry, and I could tell by his dress that he didn't go into town very often. He wore worn-out overalls with a long sleeve shirt underneath that was buttoned up to the top. He wasn't that old, but he looked older than he was. He had a couple of deep wrinkles on his forehead. It was the face of a person drinking moonshine for many years.

I looked in the back seat and noticed some kids had bruises on their arms, neck, and face. I could tell someone had been abusing them, so I put cuffs on the guy and had him sit in the back seat of my patrol car. I asked him who had put the bruises on his kids, and he wouldn't say a word. I got out of the car, looked back at him, and told him I would talk to his wife and ask her questions about the kids' going on. He immediately yelled to his wife and kids, "Don't tell him anything!" When I went to the car, I could tell they were scared to talk to me. They didn't want to tell me anything after what their dad had said. I tried to ask his wife a few questions about the bruises, and she wouldn't answer. I asked the kids why they had bruises on their arms, neck, and face in the back seat. There were three little girls and one young boy in the back. The oldest girl was around eleven or twelve years old. None of them would say a word when I asked the same questions I had asked their mother. I could tell they were more scared of their dad than I was. I asked the wife again if she or her husband had been hurting the kids. She still wouldn't answer, so I told her that I would take her and her husband to jail and charge them with child abuse if she didn't start talking. I told her that child protection services could come out and take their kids away, seeing their bruises. All four of the kids started crying when I said that.

The oldest girl slowly and reluctantly spoke up with her head down and her hands in her lap. She quietly said that their dad had done the bruises to them, not their mom. I asked her why he would do something like that to them. "Have you kids disobeyed your dad or did something he didn't want you to do?"

She sadly said, "No, sir, sometimes he likes to do nasty things to us, and if we don't do it the way he likes, he gets mad at us and beats us. She said, "Please don't take our mom to jail; it's not her fault. Please don't tell him I told you, or he will kill me if he finds out."

I asked the little girl what kind of things he did to her.

She spoke very slowly and had tears in her eyes as she said, "He makes us put his private part in our mouth, and then he puts it in our private part, and it hurts."

I asked the wife if this was true, and she very tearfully shook her head and started crying. I asked the wife if they had other kids at home, and she said no. I also asked her if anyone from her family was doing this to the kids. She shook her head no again. I promised the little girl I wouldn't tell their dad what she said. I told them I would let them go and not arrest them for anything. I told them to keep our conversation to themselves, and they agreed.

I returned to the car, reluctantly un-cuffed him, and let him go. I told him to get out of my sight before hurting him. He was not a very happy person as he drove away, cursing me and flipping me off. Typically, I wouldn't have put up with his bullcrap, but I had given his kids and wife my word that I wouldn't arrest him. I let him drive away, even though I was outraged with anger inside about what he had been doing to his kids.

I went home that night and thought about what I would do to end those poor little kids' torture. I knew there was no way the wife and kids would testify in court against him if I arrested him and put him in jail, especially if it went to trial. I also knew he would continue to do that to his poor little kids. I had to do something to stop this abuse, and I had to do it soon.

The next day, I checked in at work, drove up to where he lived, and started to see if I could figure out his daily routine. I hid my car in the woods about a half-mile from his home for him to drive by. There wasn't any traffic on the narrow dirt backwoods road the entire day. I did the same thing for the next three days until it started driving me crazy with rage.

Every day, I became more upset about that stupid child molester. I was at the point where I wanted to drive up to his house and put a bullet in his head. While waiting for him, all kinds of things went through my head. I hoped he didn't force the poor little girl or her mother to tell him what I asked them when I pulled them over. I was afraid he might beat them even more.

Finally, my plan started to come together on the afternoon of the third day. He came driving out and was alone, just like I'd hoped. By then, I could hardly contain my anger at him any longer. I pulled him over and had him get out of his car. He asked me what I was doing in his neck of the woods, harassing him. I didn't say anything to him. I hit him in the head with the Billy Club I carried in the car. He immediately fell to his knees. He started spouting garbage about how he would have me arrested for using excessive force on him. I ignored him and asked him how long he had been beating and molesting his kids. He said that was none of my damn business, "Those are my kids, and I can do whatever I want to them."

I said, "That's the wrong answer, dummy! That may be true in another county, but not in mine. Did you think I would let some low-life scum bag like you get away with molesting his kids in my county?"

He said, "What the hell do you think you'll do about it? Put me in jail? My wife and kids won't testify against me."

I replied I know that you are a piece of crap, scum bag; I am going to kill you!" He looked up at me in total shock as I hit him two more times with the Billy club, as hard as I could, on the side of the head. I kept thinking this could be Billy Joe Farris's dad that I was killing, not just some hillbilly. I heard the crunch of his busted skull from each hit of the club. He immediately went limp but was still breathing. I hit him one more time in the same spot, and he stiffened out and started jerking like one of the cats I killed when I was a kid.

After a few minutes, his breathing finally stopped. I waited a few more minutes to see if he had a pulse. Once I knew he didn't, I picked him up and threw his limp body in the front passenger side of his car. I jumped in the driver's seat of his car and buckled up. I drove the car into a big tree at about 50 miles per hour. I was a little shaken up at first, but I got out and pulled him over to the driver's side of the car like he had been driving and left the car against the tree.

I waited about 10 minutes until I calmed my nerves down and then called my office and reported the fatal car accident. I said, "Some hillbilly just ran into a tree at about 50 miles an hour, and it doesn't look like he was wearing a seat belt." They asked me if he was dead, and I said, "Yes, just send the coroner." I gave them the approximate address in the woods.

Then I drove up to his little shack in the woods and honked my horn as two big guard dogs angrily came rushing at my car, ready to attack me. After a few minutes, the hillbilly's wife very sheepishly came out of the house wearing an old dingy-looking dress with an apron wrapped around it. I told her that I had returned to check and see if her husband had gotten his taillight fixed. I found his car against a tree about a half-mile from their house. I said, "You may have heard the crash. It didn't seem too long ago that the accident might have happened." She said that she hadn't heard anything. I then broke the news that her husband was dead. She turned white as a ghost and almost fainted. I had to grab her as she stumbled toward me. I couldn't tell if she was sad or relieved about his death, but it didn't matter. All I knew was that he wouldn't be raping and beating those poor little kids anymore. I thought it also didn't matter to me that they would be without a dad and she would be without a husband. I just figured they would all be better off without him around.

I told her that I had already called the coroner's office and would be coming to pick up his body. I said I would give her a ride to the car if she wanted to see him before picking him up. She said she would rather stay with the kids. I told her I would return in about three days and check on them to see if they were doing okay. She said that would be fine and turned back into the house.

I knew I had to come back soon because I wanted to ensure no one else in the family was abusive to those kids. No uncles or cousins or other scum bags hanging around. I returned to the car and waited for the coroner to pick up the body. While sitting there by myself waiting, I said, you shouldn't have been such a nasty and belligerent person. Maybe I wouldn't have killed you and only hurt you instead. Maybe not! I don't think I would've done anything differently!

Once the coroner arrived and I left the scene, I felt that old familiar rush again. All the way home that night, I couldn't stop thinking that poor sucker had gotten what he had come for.

RON L. CARTER

***

Chapter 11- Spencer's killed

A few years passed, and things went smoothly for Cori, me, and Jason. We were enjoying our life together, and we were happy. I got a call from my youngest son, Travis, who was 15 then. He told me that my oldest son Spencer was dead.

I didn't have a favorite son, but Spencer was my firstborn, and I did have a special attachment to him. I asked Travis what had happened, but he was too upset to go into it on the phone. Travis did say that two boys from a Mexican gang killed Spencer, but that's all Travis would say. He said he would tell me all about it when I got there.

I immediately made arrangements with work, let Cori know what was happening, and headed to California. The entire way there, a million things were running through my mind. I had heard about Mexican gangs before, but I thought they were mainly in big cities like Los Angeles or New York. I would've never guessed that some gang members could've killed my son.

I had tons of emotions driving me crazy as I made the drive. It felt like that drive was taking me forever to get there. For some reason, I felt very alone and sad, almost like I did growing up. I had to pull the car over, get out, and walk around to stop the tears pouring down my face a few times.

I felt guilty about not spending more time with my boys; now, it was killing me inside. I tried to justify why I had left them when they were so young. I was trying to tell myself it was because I didn't want to take them away from their mother. I could try to fool myself, but I knew it had nothing to do with that deep down inside. I didn't want to be responsible for raising kids at that time. I knew I wouldn't make a good father or husband, and I wasn't in love with their mother. I would've been doing to them what mom and dad did to us, just fighting and arguing all the time. Now, I was feeling like a bad father. I wasn't there to watch my sons grow up or protect them from the evil in the world.

Even though I had hurt and killed a few people, I always felt like each deserved what they got. I didn't feel like a 16-year-old kid deserved to die at the hands of some gang members.

The closer I got to California, the deeper my hurt and rage became. I knew I wouldn't let those punks get away with killing my boy. I had to restrain my feelings when I met Travis and his mom.

We went through the usual motions when you lose someone close to you and love so deeply. It was a weird next three days, spending time with them, making arrangements, and going to the funeral.

I could find out precisely from Travis what had happened during that time. He said Spencer liked this little Mexican girl about the same age as Spencer. They had been sneaking around and spending a lot of time together. She had dated a Mexican boy a few times before she met Spencer, and he was in a gang. They were sneaking around out of fear and retaliation from this boy and his gang members. She said he had threatened her and warned her not to go out with Spencer.

Travis said that Spencer kept getting braver about being with her and would walk her home after school. Sometimes, they would stop in the park on the way home and make out. The Mexican kid saw them together in the park, which made him angry. Spencer told Travis that the Mexican kid had threatened him a few times and told him to stay away from his girlfriend. Spencer didn't take the threat seriously, and the last time the guy threatened him, he got into a fistfight at school. Some guys broke it up, and Spencer thought it was all over because he didn't have any trouble with the kid after that. At least not until the day they killed him.

Spencer's Mexican girlfriend was at the funeral, so I had a chance to sit down and talk with her. She was very broken up over the whole thing and felt guilty for what had happened. I told her it wasn't her fault and that Spencer must have cared much about her if he was willing to fight her ex-boyfriend over her. Between the tears, I discovered the boy's name and the friend she thought helped him kill Spencer.

After the funeral, I went to the local police department and introduced myself as a Sherriff from Arkansas. I told them that some Mexican gang members had killed my son Spencer a few days earlier. I gave them the names of the boys I got from Spencer's girlfriend that she thought killed him. According to everyone who knew my son and his girlfriend, I told them we were pretty sure these were the two guys who had pulled the trigger. I told them the ex-boyfriend's name was Jose Miguel Garcia. He lived with his family in a small house on the north/west side of town. He was the oldest kid in the family. I told them he was pretty involved with a Mexican gang, but I didn't know.

The other boy involved in my son's murder was Jose's best friend, Carlos Martinez. Since early childhood, they had been friends, and he lived with his mom and dad and a couple of younger sisters just a few streets over from Jose. His dad was a farm labor worker who worked in the fields. From what I was hearing, I don't think his dad was too involved in his son's life. Maybe he just gave up and couldn't control his son anymore after becoming part of the gang.

The police told me that there were no witnesses to the murder of my son and that it would be hard to convict the two boys. They said they would have to have someone come forward who saw what happened to do anything about it. I already knew that would be the answer, but I just wanted the police to try and see what they could do to solve my son's murder. I knew these boys would pay for my son's death one way or another.

I stayed for an extra week with my son Travis and his mom, just trying to give them some comfort, but most importantly, I was finding out more and more about the gang and Jose and Carlos. I found out where Jose lived, and I staked out his house. I soon became very familiar with his routine.

I knew his appearance and how he walked and watched his every move. I found out when he left during the day and when he came home at night. I found out what days he would be alone. I did the same thing with Carlos. I found out what he looked like and where he lived.

One day, when they were both together and watching them, I whispered, *boys, your days are numbered*. However, I knew I would be the number one suspect if I killed them while still in town. I decided to return to Arkansas and let things cool off.

During that cooling-off period, I devised a plan and started formulating what I would do in my mind. I decided to put my list into action on the next four-day weekend. I told Cori I was going to California to take care of some business. She knew what business I was talking about but never said anything. She had learned a long time ago that once I made my mind up to something, there was nothing anyone could do to talk me out of it. I told her that if anyone called asking for me while I was gone, tell them I had gone deer hunting.

I left on a Wednesday after I got off work and headed for California. I figured I could make it there in 34 hours if I drove straight through, only stopping for gas. I used cash to pay for my gas, and Cori cut my hair shorter than average. I wore a baseball cap and sunglasses to hide my identity somewhat. That was different than the usual cowboy hat I usually wore.

When I got to my son's hometown in California, I spent a few hours sleeping in my car before doing anything. I also wanted to lay low and observe my targets for several hours. I never let Travis, his mom, or anyone else know I was in California. I had brought a 12-gauge shotgun that I had taken from our confiscated weapons room at work. I was going to use it to kill the boys. I learned from law enforcement that a shotgun was the most complicated weapon to trace back to the one that used it. One of the only ways to find the killer is to get caught with the gun in your possession. And have some of the shells on you.

That evening, I waited until it was dark and thought I knew when Jose would come home, according to my last calculations. My timing was right because it was around 11:00 pm when he finally came driving in alone. I recognized his car as he parked it in the street. I pulled up opposite him on the other side of the road. I made sure it was him as he got out of the car. I stuck the shotgun out of the car window and took quick aim. I shot him once in the head and once in the chest from that close range. I didn't have to check him; I knew he was dead. He went down without even a sound. I watched his body squirm on the ground, gasping for his last breath before I left. I said *I got you, punk; you're dead now.*

Then, I quickly headed over to Carlos's house. His car was parked out front, so I knew he must be home. I waited for him to come out, thinking he would be heading over to Jose's house once he got word of Jose's death. I figured that if he didn't come out within a half-hour, I would just let him go until I could return and finish my plan another time.

It was just as I thought, and I didn't have to wait too long. Carlos came flying out of the house, carrying a gun with him. As soon as I saw him exit the front door and start heading for his car, I knew it was him. Just before he got in his car, I started driving past him. As he reached his car, I stopped, stuck the shotgun out of the window, and shot him twice at close range. He shot him in the back of the head and the other one in his back. I didn't waste any time as I headed out of the area, as nothing had happened.

As I left, I thought those two punks would never kill anyone else again. They got what was coming to them.

I headed back to Arkansas without anyone ever knowing that I had even been in California. I was pumped up from the adrenaline rush most of the way around. That made it an easy drive home for me. I didn't sleep the entire way. I made it to Arkansas by Sunday night but was exhausted from no sleep when I got home. Luckily, Monday was a holiday, and I could sleep all day.

When I returned to work on Tuesday, I waited until everyone was at lunch, and then I slipped the shotgun back into the evidence room. No one would know that the gun killed the two guys in California. My plan was complete.

That Tuesday afternoon, I got a call at my office from the police department in the little town in California where Spencer died. The police officer informed me that the two boy suspects of my son's death were dead. I asked him how it happened, and he told me it looked like a drive-by shooting. He said they thought it might have been members from another rival gang. I told the police officer I wasn't disappointed to hear that it had happened to them, and he said he could understand my feelings.

That was the entire conversation, and the call lasted only a few minutes. I also think the officer was checking to see if I was in Arkansas. I thought he was slightly surprised when I answered my phone at work. I was probably one of their significant suspects before he talked to me. I never got a call from anyone after that conversation, so my plan must have worked. They didn't investigate me for the two murders.

Travis called me a few days later to tell me someone had killed the two boys. I told him the police had already called me and notified me, but thanked him anyway. I told him I was happy because I thought they deserved what they deserved. He agreed with me.

***

Chapter 12 - Meeting Frank Callahan

I got a call from one of the mayors of a small town in my county called Clarksville. It was located between Mena and Norman and was up in the Ouachita Mountain's most wooded part. He said he wanted me to talk to him about some folks living in the woods and brewing moonshine. I didn't know much about moonshiners except those who made the whiskey's descendants were from Scotland or Ireland in the 1700s. They brought their whiskey-making ways and settled throughout the hills in the south. They developed their way of talking in America, and that's why they had what I thought was such an unusual southern accent. They set their way of speaking English with their Scottish and Irish accents, which always sounded long and drawn out to me.

Before I hung up the phone, I told the mayor I would meet him the next day at his office. It was over an hour's drive, but I met with him there. During our conversation, he told me some hillbilly folks lived further up in the woods. They were located down a dirt road and hidden away from everyone. I asked him, "What's your problem with them?" He said that one of the families had three boys in their late teens and early twenties, and they had been giving moonshine to some of the young high school girls in town. They were also selling it to some of the boys in town.

One of the boys sold some moonshine to a local high school kid who got drunk. He ended up beating up and raping a girl from his school while drunk. I told the mayor that it could have happened regardless of the moonshine. He said, "I know, but the guy whose daughter was beaten up and raped beat up the kid that did it and almost killed him. He also told me that he would take the law into his own hands if I didn't have something done about those Damn hillbillies and their moonshine."

I asked, "What exactly do you want me to do?"

He said, "I don't want you to cause any trouble; I need you to tell the boys to lay low and stay away from town until this whole thing blows over. You must be careful when you go up there because they have guns. They might kill you if they feel you're a threat to them or their moonshine. They seem to follow their law up in those hills." I told him I would take care of it, call him in a few days, and tell him how it went.

I wasn't sure what I was getting myself into, but I immediately headed to their place. When I first got there, I saw that they had no electricity coming into the home and no running water. It looked like they just pumped their water from a well and used oil lamps for light. They had outhouses for toilets behind the two little brown shacks that appeared to be about 200 years old. You could tell they needed paint. Clothes were hanging on a couple of lines. Each house had front porches where it looked like they spent much of their time. There were several homemade chairs and rocking chairs out on the porches. The place was clean around the yard, and there was a big fire pit made of rocks between both houses. It had a light smoke ring that slowly drifted out as it faded into the sky. I could smell the smoke in the air, and the sweet smell of the Hickory and Pine drifted through the trees. They used this pit a lot because of all the logs and homemade chairs surrounding the rock formation. This entire area was dry and had no lawn or flowers. It was just natural vegetation and trees. It reminded me of a large, double campsite.

As soon as I drove in with my patrol car, four big Red Tick and Blue Tick Hounds came barking up to meet me, and they didn't seem too friendly. I was hoping that the owner of this place was a little more hospitable. I soon learned I was wrong; the owner stepped out of his house with a rifle. As I slowly opened my car door, I could see three other men with rifles in their hands pointed at me.

I could tell that these guys had no respect for the law and would kill me if I made any wrong moves. With my right hand, I raised my hands in the air and slowly took the pistol from my holster, showed it to them, and then tossed it on the front seat of my car.

I yelled at the guy on the porch and asked him if he was Mr. Frank Callahan. He nodded his head yes. I told him that I was County Sherriff Walker and that Mayor Stonewall had asked me to come and talk to him about his boys. I asked him if he would talk to me for a few minutes. When I said something about his boys, I got his attention, so he motioned me to come forward. He yelled something to the dogs, and as soon as he spoke, the dogs immediately walked away and found a place to lie down.

I slowly walked up to the porch with my hands still in the air. I wasn't going to take any chances with these guys.

As I approached him, he said, "What do you want with my boys?"

I replied, "Do you mind if we just sit for a minute to talk?" He told me to put my hands down and join him in one of the chairs on the porch. He wasn't that old, but he had wrinkles and lines on his face from what I thought was a rough life. Maybe it was from the years of smoking and drinking moonshine.

Once we passed the formalities and he saw I wasn't a threat, the three young guys slowly approached me. He told the boys everything was okay, and I just wanted to talk. They put down their guns when he said that. I began to tell him what Mayor Stonewall had told me about the girls getting moonshine from his boys and selling it to some of the kids in town. I told him about the girl's incident, and the girl's father was putting heat on the mayor to do something about his boys and their moonshine.

When I told him the story, he got angry and had all three boys join us on the porch. I introduced myself to them and repeated the story. Of course, their first reaction was denial and anger. I calmly told them there was no need to get defensive about their role in what I was saying. I'm not here to arrest anyone. I said, "We must solve the mayor's problem."

I told them that the mayor told me he thought it would be better if the boys were to stay out of town for a while. Stay close to home and avoid being seen in town with any girls or moonshine. He felt the most important thing was not to sell moonshine to the local boys until this thing blew over. The mayor also said he couldn't guarantee the boys' safety if they didn't do what he asked. He suggested the boys go to another town if they wanted to meet girls and sell their moonshine.

I could tell Mr. Callahan was unaware that his boys had been selling the moonshine to the kids in town or giving it to any of the girls. When I talked about it, he didn't say anything. He just had his piercing and angry eyes glare from one son to the next. There wasn't any doubt with any of us that he wasn't happy. It appeared to me that he might have had this conversation with the boys before.

I thought, any minute now, he would jump and start beating and cursing the boys. I knew these boys would be in big trouble once I left, so I didn't have to say much more about it.

I told Mr. Callahan that I was aware of his moonshine stills and that I didn't have a problem with it if he didn't put me in a position to do something about it (like a mayor telling me to do something else). He understood what I meant. I told him he didn't need this kind of attention for himself and his "livelihood." Especially since he was doing something illegal in the eyes of the law, he said, "I appreciate you coming and talking to me about this. I'll take care of things with my boys. I damn well guarantee you that."

I replied nothing more needed to be said, "I figured you would."

I then changed the subject and started talking about other things. I asked Mr. Callahan about his hound dogs and if he used them for hunting raccoons. He said yes, "We go coon hunting just about every few weeks. My dogs are the best "coon hounds in the country." I told him that I had gone "coon" hunting when I was younger, with my uncles, who lived near Caddo-Gap, Arkansas. He asked me if I liked it, and I told him I did. I thought it was a lot of fun. He said we don't do it for fun. We do it to sell their skins and get things we need from town. If you agree, you can go with us anytime." I told him I would like to take my son, Jason, along with us if he was okay. He replied, "Sure, that wouldn't be a problem. Just let me know when." Soon, we were all laughing and talking, and I realized how much I enjoyed my conversation with him and his boys.

After we had all become friends, Mr. Callahan offered me a drink of his moonshine. I told him that I had heard about moonshine but never tasted it. He had one of the boys get a jug of his finest. They brought out a few mason jars and poured us a drink. We toasted one another, and I took a big swig, about the size of two shot glasses. I didn't realize it was around 180 proof and almost pure alcohol. The moment it reached my tongue, it burned as I had just swallowed a ball of fire, and even worse, as it went down. I could feel the stuff every inch of the way until it hit my stomach. It sat in my stomach and burned like I had eaten hot chili peppers. The first thought that crossed my mind was of the cat I had poured liniment on its butt when I was a kid. When I was young, I knew that cat's butt must have burned just like the moonshine did as it blazed a trail down my throat. I had never tasted anything like this before in my life. I thought it might almost be like drinking pure rubbing alcohol.

I wondered how those young girls from town could stand drinking the stuff. If I wanted to get high, I'd much rather just smoke pot than put up with burning out my guts.

I stayed for another hour and had about a quarter of a jar of that "rotgut alcohol." When I got ready to leave, I thanked Mr. Callahan and the boys and returned to my car. I was having trouble walking straight and realized I was almost drunk. They were all laughing at me as I left. Mr. Callahan said, "You're welcome up here anytime, Sherriff." I thanked him for his hospitality, time, and moonshine.

As I headed out of his place, I decided I'd better pull over in the woods someplace down the road and sleep it off for a few hours. I knew that I had no business driving home drunk. I didn't want to end up crashing into a tree or, even worse, into another car and killing myself or a few people. After a few hours of sleep, I could get home without problems.

A few days later, I called Mayor Stonewall and told him I had handled everything with the Callahan boys. I told him he wouldn't have any more trouble with them. He thanked me and said he was happy to hear I had everything under control.

***

Chapter 13 - Sweet Becky of Las Vegas

A few days later, I received a note from the Mayor of Broken Arrow. He said they required me to attend a four-day convention in Las Vegas. It was a requirement for all law enforcement officers. It was during the week. They would be talking about sexual harassment in the workplace. Quite a few lawsuits have started to pop up worldwide regarding police officers making advances toward the girls working in the offices, especially toward female officers.

They planned for me at the Flamingo Hotel on the Las Vegas strip. All the rooms and meals are taken care of for the three nights. They also paid for our gas or flights, whichever I chose, to get me there and back. It was supposed to be a big event, with hundreds in attendance each day. I hoped this would be a rare trip where I could bring Cori. We could have a great time after the meetings each day. We could go to a few shows, and she could gamble a little. It would be great for the two of us, like a vacation.

When I discussed it with her, she said she couldn't go. It happened to be the time of year when Jason was in school. We didn't know anyone we trusted enough to watch Jason. She still feared that her ex-husband might have someone show up and take him back to California. After we discussed it, and much to my disappointment, I would go alone. I had never been in an airplane before, and I had a slight fear of flying. I decided I would take my pick-up and drive to Las Vegas.

I was excited to get away for a few days when the time came. I never had a company pay for me to stay in a hotel, plus all my expenses. I was looking forward to it. On the drive there, I became more excited the closer I got to Vegas.

Once I arrived at the Flamingo, it was even better than I'd imagined. It was a vast place, and when I went to check-in, the valet asked me if I wanted them to park my pick-up. I said, "Sure," as I grabbed my suitcase from the truck's passenger side. I had only brought one bag for the entire trip. I gave the bellman a few bucks to park my vehicle, and he gave me a ticket with a number.

I couldn't believe the excitement when I first entered the hotel-casino. I could hear slot machines going off, people talking loudly, and other noises. It made me feel like I was in the middle of a huge party. This place rushed me, like when I had stolen something or beaten some guy up. I wasn't much of a gambler, although, on a few occasions, I used to play stud poker with Buddy. I knew I wouldn't gamble too much because I didn't particularly appreciate losing money. I felt that money belonged to Cori and me and didn't want to lose it gambling.

After checking in and receiving my key, I took my suitcase to the room. I had a massive room with two queen beds. After I put my clothes away and stuck the bag in the closet, I decided to head downstairs to check the place out. I couldn't believe how big the casino was; it was alive, and everything was in perfect harmony. There were tons of slot machines everywhere you looked, all making noises. They were up against the walls, around the middle of the floor. There were also tons of Blackjack tables, Roulette tables, Kino areas, and several bars.

They were so busy gambling that they didn't even look up to see what else was happening around them. Young servers dressed in skimpy little outfits were scurrying around carrying drinks to different tables. This place was crazy, and I loved it!

At first, I didn't know what to do with myself, but I remembered passing a bar while walking through the casino. I decided to go back there, have a few drinks, and kill some time. I sat there and took it all in for a while. After a few drinks, I realized it was getting a little late, and I was tired from the long drive, so I decided to return to my room. Once I returned to the room, I called Cori and told her what a crazy place this was. I wished she had come with me. I told her that someday we would have to make this trip together. She agreed. I told her I loved her, and we said our goodnights.

I called the front desk and found out when the meeting would occur. The operator said they could give me a wake-up call. I lie on the bed, turn on the T.V., and soon, fast asleep.

The next thing I knew, the front desk called to wake me up, just as I had requested. I got up, showered, and put on my most excellent jeans, a long white sleeve shirt, and the cowboy boots I had polished before packing for Vegas. I was feeling good about how I felt and looked. I went downstairs to get some breakfast and coffee before the meeting.

When I got to the meeting, it was packed. There were tons of people, primarily men, dressed in suits. Some even wore nice slacks, sports coats, and ties. I felt a little awkward for not being dressed like them. After I found a seat at one of the tables, I introduced myself and sat down.

As I began conversing with the guys at the table, I realized we were all in the same boat. Everyone was a little nervous.

I looked around the room, and there weren't many women in attendance, but one was at my table. She is petite, attractive, young, and the type of woman I find appealing.

She held a professional, costly camera and looked nervously around the room. Occasionally, she would glance at me, smile, and quickly turn away. It seemed by her actions that she liked me. I was wearing a wedding ring on my finger, and I wasn't trying to hide the fact that I was married. I wasn't trying to hide anything. I enjoyed her attention but couldn't help thinking *why a well-dressed and, I assumed, well-educated lady like her would be interested in a cowboy like me.*

I told her my name was Cody. She said her name was Becky.

She giggled and said, "Is that like, "Buffalo Bill" Cody?

I said, "exactly," and we both laughed. Becky then got up and started taking pictures of different people in the room.

The meeting finally started, and it wasn't exciting, but I did my best to sit through it without getting up and walking out. I was very relieved when we finally broke up for lunch. We made small talk as we ate. After a few minutes, Becky came over and sat down to eat. She asked me where I was from, how long I had been married, and how many kids I had. The usual things you ask someone when you're interested in them. I played it very cool, trying hard not to give her any "come on" signals. The more I ignored her, the more questions she asked me.

She started telling me about herself and her work. She told me that she was a local photographer hired to take pictures of the convention. They would send out a souvenir publication with all the pictures she took to attendees. She said she was single, had no kids, and lived alone with her little dog in Las Vegas. She said one of her jobs was taking pictures of the tourists visiting the Hoover Dam. She said, "It's only about forty-five minutes from Vegas, and it's beautiful to see." She was entertaining and exciting.

The meeting started again and went on until about 4:45 that afternoon. I was glad when it was over, but I was dreading that there would be two more days of this boring stuff.

Some of the guys from my table said they were going to the bar, so I joined them. As we all got up and headed over, I told Becky we would see her tomorrow.

We'd been at the bar for about an hour, laughing and telling jokes, when Becky walked up and asked if she could join us. We said sure; we didn't mind having her around. Besides, she was easy on the eyes. After a while, we were all hungry, so we decided to go to the buffet and have dinner.

Becky left and went to join some other people she'd already made plans with for dinner.

After dinner, I decided to go to the bar and drink a few more. It was getting late, and I'd finally had enough to drink. I knew that I needed to go to bed, or I'd never be able to get up for the meeting the next day. I was trying to get in when I got to my room.

Just as I opened the door and walked into my room, I heard this sexy female voice say, "Hey cowboy, wait up." It was from Becky. She shut the door and strolled into my room before I realized what was happening. She also had too much to drink as she said, "I figured you could use some company. I know I sure could. Do you have anything to drink?"

I looked around the room and said, "No, it doesn't look like it."

She said, "Oh well, it's your lucky day, cowboy," as she started taking off her clothes and heading for my bed.

I was starting to see a different side to the sweet, innocent girl I had met downstairs. I thought, what the hell is she doing? I told her that I had to go to the bathroom, but she was lying naked on my bed when I got out. One look at her nude body poised to show off her incredibly sexy, petite figure, and I knew there was no more turning back for me. I'm not sure if it was because I'd also had too much to drink or because she was so inviting, but I started tearing off my clothes, and by then, she had her breasts pressed up against my body.

I could feel her nipples harden as she leaned up and kissed me. As soon as she did that, I started to get turned on. I ran my hands down her back and squeezed her firm butt cheeks with the palm of my hands. I kissed her deeply and hard, bent over, and kissed her very softly on the left side of her neck. I gently ran the tip of my tongue up her neck and around the outside of her left ear. She started squirming and said she couldn't take it anymore. It all felt so good that, for a moment, I even forgot who or where I was. I sure wasn't thinking about being married.

We went at it for about thirty minutes, and afterward, we stayed curled up in each other's arms and kissed for a while. In my somewhat drunken stupor, I thought it was nice to have sex with Becky.

Then, something strange happened to her, and her mood immediately changed. She stood up and said, "I like you, cowboy, and

I loved having sex with you, so from now on, YOU ARE MINE." At first, I thought she was kidding around, and I laughed. I soon learned she wasn't joking and started saying pretty weird things: "Once someone sleeps with me, they are mine until I let them go. I know your wife's name is Cori, and you have a son named Jason. You live in Broken Arrow, Arkansas." I knew she probably got that information from the bio card I had filled out, but I didn't know how she got her hands on it. She said, "You're MY man from now on. Call your wife now and tell her you want to have a new girl." Those words instantly made me start to sober up quickly.

I sat in bed and said, "Hey, Becky, you knew I was married before you came into my room, and we had sex." She seemed offended when I said that, and she replied, "What do you mean? You made love to me; you've been watching me all day. You wanted me, too, I could tell." I tried to be very gentle with her because I realized anything I said wrong might set her off in her state of mind. I told her I found her very attractive and loved having sex with her, but we didn't make love. WE JUST HAD SEX. I told her it was "raw sex to me, and that was all it was and nothing more." I told her I wasn't looking for someone to replace my wife.

At that point, she started getting agitated and way out of control. She said she would call Cori and tell her that I had sex with her while at the Las Vegas convention. I didn't understand what was happening with her and where this was heading.

I tried hard to talk to her and calm her down, but I couldn't reason with her no matter what I said. She was like a completely different person. I said I thought she was sweet and just looking for a one-night stand, and I was the guy she wanted. She said, "Do you think I do this with every guy I meet?"

I replied, "I don't know. I just met you, so I haven't had a chance to form an opinion of you. I believe you're a nice person, and based on what I've seen of you, no, I don't believe you have sex with every person you meet." I could tell she wasn't buying my answers and kept getting louder and angrier by the moment. I now understood why she was still single. For a second time, she said she would call and tell Cori that I had sex with her in Las Vegas, which started to scare me and make me very angry.

It had very quickly turned into a nightmare for me. When Becky said it the second time, it was almost more than I could stand, and I could no longer control my temper. I snapped and hit her as hard as I could on the left side of the temple with my closed fist. She went down like one of the deer I had shot and killed back home.

I instantly realized there was no turning back after I hit her that first time. I'd have to kill her to keep her quiet. Before I realized what I was doing, I hit her three or four more times on the same side of the head as hard as I could. She started jerking and gasping for air, and in a minute, she went silent. Just like that, she lay dead in my hotel room. I felt for a pulse but couldn't get one.

I didn't want to kill her, but she pushed the wrong buttons with me. I was pumped up and still angry as I sat on the bed and tried to figure out what I would do next. I had to figure out how to get her out of my room and out of the hotel without anyone seeing me take her body out. As I was trying to figure it out, I noticed she had brought her purse and camera and thrown them into a corner of my room. I looked through her bag and found her wallet and ID. I found her address and keys to her car and house.

I rechecked her to ensure she was dead and then picked her up and laid her back on the bed. I grabbed her keys and went down to the parking garage. After about a half-hour of searching, I finally found her car. I drove it out and parked it a few blocks away in a dark area. I then returned to my room, dumped everything out of my suitcase, and tried to put her body in it, but it wasn't big enough. I'd hoped her body would fit in it, but it was too small. I decided to have a large suitcase, so I left her in the room again and looked for one.

I left the hotel and walked down the street toward some of the larger, busier hotels. People were checking in and out at all hours of the day and night. I spotted a suitcase just the size I needed, sitting alone outside the hotel. I waited a few minutes to see if someone was watching it. I didn't see anyone, so I casually grabbed the handle and strolled back to my hotel. The entire way back, I kept looking over my shoulder to be sure no one was following me. I dumped everything in the suitcase in a dumpster before taking it to my room.

It looked like it was just big enough for her body, so I carefully took her nude body, folded it into a fetal position, and stuffed her clothes, camera, and purse in the suitcase. It was tight, but I was able to zip it up. You couldn't tell there was a body in it. I could still pull the suitcase and not have to carry it.

It can get cold at night in Las Vegas during that time of year, so I threw my coat over the suitcase to camouflage it a little. I also knew I would have to walk back to the hotel once I disposed of her body, so I needed something to keep me warm. I took the suitcase and left the room as I walked down the elevator and back entrance. I went down the street to her car, popped open the trunk, lifted the suitcase, and put it in. I planned to take her to Hoover Dam and throw her and everything over the cliff. The only problem was that I couldn't figure out how to get back to Las Vegas without catching a cab or some other ride. Those witnesses could've tied me to the location and possibly her body.

Now the big question was, what do I do with her body? After several minutes of contemplation, I drove to her house and left her there. She lived in a friendly, inexpensive neighborhood about ten miles from the Flamingo Hotel. I found my way to her home and waited until it looked like most of her neighbor's lights were out and it was safe. I then drove into her driveway with the lights off. I slipped into the house through the front door to ensure the lights were off. I opened the garage door and quickly drove her car in and parked.

After removing the suitcase from the trunk, I took it inside and into the main bathroom. I took her body and placed it in her main bedroom tub. I wanted it to look like she had gotten ready to take a bath, slipped, and hit her head on the side.

While waiting for the bathtub to fill, I searched for bleach. I found a half-full bottle under the kitchen sink. Before I dumped Becky's body in the tub, I emptied the bottle of bleach in the water. I'd heard that bleach gets rid of the evidence. I let her soak for about 10 minutes, drained the water, and filled it again. I used some of the foamy soap she had for her baths this time.

At first glance and to the untrained eye, it appeared that she had slipped, hit her head on the tub, and drowned. I figured that when the coroner found the blows to the side of her head, they would think she got them when she fell. If they thought she got murdered, it would be hard to pin it on me because no one ever saw us alone. We were always with other people.

I went around and wiped all the places I had touched, including the car, the keys, and the steering wheel, and grabbed my coat from the car. I wiped down the bleach bottle and put it back under the sink. I went into her bedroom closet, found a nightgown she had hanging, and put it on the toilet next to the bathtub. I took her clothes out of the suitcase and threw them on the bed as if she had just taken them off and gone to take a bath. I locked the front door from the inside, and after wiping them clean, I left her keys and camera on the kitchen table.

After surveying the room, I thought everything looked normal as I left. I took the suitcase out of the garage side door to the backyard and locked everything behind me.

I started walking back to the hotel, the suitcase dragging behind me. Whenever I saw car lights coming my way, I would hide in some bushes until they passed. After several minutes, I could find a dumpster and throw the suitcase. I returned to the hotel and got back around 3:00 in the morning.

After a couple of hours of sleep, I was back up and on my way to the meeting. I followed the plan for two days, and no one noticed anything unusual. The rest of my time there was uneventful. Someone came to our table and asked if we'd seen Becky, and everyone said no.

I was a little anxious about getting out of there. I packed my suitcase and headed down to the lobby to check out. The valet pulled my truck around to the front entrance; I tipped him a few dollars, drove away, and never looked back.

I couldn't wait to see Cori and Jason on the way home. While driving, I thought *I liked Becky and didn't want to kill her, but she was a total fruitcake and should never have threatened me. If she had kept her mouth shut, none of that would've happened to her.* I never heard anything more regarding Becky.

***

Chapter 14 - Meeting Bruce and Kathy Tuttle

A few days after I was home from Las Vegas, I had coffee with Cori early in the morning before work. She told me that since Jason was in school, she felt like she needed something to do besides sit home alone all day. She talked to me about the new factory opening in Queensland. She said she had spoken to them about going to work for them while I was in Vegas. At first, I was against it because I made enough money to care for our family. I didn't like the idea of my wife working because I always felt it was my job to care for her and Jason. We went back and forth about it for a few days until I reluctantly gave in to her wishes. She made me realize it wasn't about the money but more about having self-worth and feeling good about herself besides being a wife and a mother.

At first, when she went to work, I missed having her at home. I missed her company and taking care of Jason and my every need, but when she got her first paycheck, I could see how happy and excited she was to contribute to the family income. Even though I was still not too fond of her work, I slowly began to accept the idea.

One day, she came home and said she had met a friendly family at the local grocery store, where she stopped after work. Their names were Bruce and Kathy Tuttle. They were about our age and had two daughters, Ashley and Stephanie, who were the same age as Jason. She said that they were friendly and seemed like very nice people. Cori said that she thought I would like Bruce a lot because he seemed like a nice guy. She went on to say that Kathy's grandmother was old Ms. Fisher, who had passed away a few months earlier, and she had left her farm to Kathy. The farm was just a few miles down the road from our place.

Kathy said that she had spent almost every summer with her grandmother from around ten years old until she married Bruce right after high school. She told Cori that she loved the old farm. Bruce had lost his job in Hot Springs a few months earlier, so they decided to move to the farm and try to live the simple country life with no mortgage payments. Her girls weren't thrilled with the move but seemed to be adjusting.

Cori told them we loved that place, and every time we drove by that old farm, we wondered what the house looked like inside. She told Cori they would invite us for a BBQ after getting things a little more organized, and we could see the place ourselves. Cori asked if that would be all right with me. I was very apprehensive initially because we hadn't socialized with anyone since we moved to Broken Arrow. We kept to ourselves out of fear of someone finding out we'd kidnapped Jason. I didn't want Cori to face charges and go to jail.

The only visitors were my mom, who would visit occasionally. She would stay about 2 or 3 days and then go back home. That was fine with me because I didn't particularly appreciate having her around for much longer than that. She wasn't married or with anyone and lived alone in Little Rock, Arkansas.

My brothers each lived in small towns in Oklahoma and would visit us occasionally. They usually just stayed for the day and then drove back home. That had been the extent of our social life with no outside friends.

I've never been crazy about making new friends, even before I was with Cori. After being with her, I wouldn't say I liked how men would gawk and act stupid around her. Since Cori showed genuine interest in Kathy and was excited about possibly having a new friend to talk to and confide in, I told her that I thought it might be good for us to make some new friends. I did it mainly to satisfy Cori because it didn't matter. We'd lived there for a few years, and no one had discovered our secret. I told Cori she should accept the next time Kathy invited us to a BBQ.

When I got home from work, Cori told me she had seen Kathy at the store again a few weeks later. She and her husband wanted us to attend a BBQ on Saturday at about 4:00 pm. We both agreed it would be okay and made plans to go to their house.

When we first drove up to their house, I saw a bubbly and excited woman come running from inside her house and practically bounce up to Cori. She smiled from ear to ear as she hugged Cori and Jason. She said, "Thank you for coming; we are so excited to have you guys over." Kathy was about five'4" with short blond hair. An inch or so of darker roots were growing out. She had a pretty smile, and with her warm personality, I felt relaxed and welcomed by her. She was a little chubby for my taste, but I could tell she had been lovely once. She reminded me of some of the cheerleaders from my high school days. As I slowly approached her, she stuck out her hand to shake mine and said, "You must be Cody?"

After the introduction of formalities, I followed them into the house. That's when I met Bruce Tuttle. He was a nice-looking guy about my size, only a little more muscular. He looked like he could've been a running back for the football team in high school. He had long, wavy black hair, a little greying around the temples, and a "Colgate" smile. For a moment, I stepped back and thought, *I don't know if I want Cori around this guy. He's a little too good-looking to be hanging out with her.* Then he shook my hand and said, "Hi, I'm Bruce. Thanks for coming. What can I get you to drink?"

I said, "I'll take a beer, a Jack and Coke, or whatever you have."

He made me a Jack and Coke, saying, "Come on outside, and we'll let those girls talk while we BBQ the meat."

Jason was a little shy and didn't want to hang out with his mom and all the girls, so he returned with us. He was being a little standoffish around Bruce and kept a guarded attitude toward him. We grabbed the folding chairs Bruce had by the BBQ and began to get to know each other. The more he talked, the more I liked him. We had a lot of similarities. He told me that he came from a broken home and that his mom and dad had gotten a divorce when he was about eleven or twelve, just like me. He said his mom had raised him, and his dad remarried a few years after the divorce. He said he still got to see his dad as often as he wanted because they all lived in the same town. He told me he played football in high school but was the quarterback, not the running back. He said that he and Kathy met in high school, and they started dating their senior year. She got pregnant right after they graduated high school, which ended their college plans. He said he didn't regret anything; he has two beautiful daughters and a beautiful wife. He said he and Kathy were happy and still in love even after their years together.

I asked him if he liked to hunt and fish and had ever been "coon" hunting? He said he had never done any of those things but would like to try them someday. He said he had a county job as a building inspector in Hot Springs for 18 years and had no friends who did that. I told him that Jason and I go fishing and hunting every chance we get. He said, "I thought you could only hunt deer in season."

I smirked and replied, "That's true, but when you're the county Sherriff, you can get away with a few things now and then. I hunt when I want to." We all just laughed when I said that. I told him that Arkansas has some of the best fishing and hunting areas in the United States. I suggested that since he wasn't working, I could teach him how to hunt deer and fish on my days off.

He seemed very excited about the idea, saying, "I would love to start doing something like that."

I asked him what he planned to do for work, and he said that when he lost his job, they gave him a good severance package and that Bruce didn't have to work for a while if he didn't want to. He said, "We don't owe anything on the farm, so that helps. I can afford to take my time and look around for something I'd like to do."

We spent the rest of the day talking and getting to know each other. I was starting to like Bruce, and Kathy was also lovely. While sitting outside, Kathy said, "We should make this a regular thing. Maybe we could also play cards or something after eating?" Cori and I both thought that sounded like a great idea. When we got ready to leave, I walked out to the truck, and Cori said goodbye to Bruce and the girls. Kathy said, "I am sure glad we ran into Cori at the store and invited you guys to our house."

To my surprise, we had a great time with them. Cori said she liked Bruce and Kathy and was glad we had made friends on the ride home. I felt the same way and looked forward to meeting them again. I hadn't had a close friend since Buddy, and I used to hang out, and that was several years ago.

Cori started hanging out with Kathy on her days off work, and it seemed like they were together practically all the time on the weekends. If Cori wasn't at her house, Kathy was at ours. Kathy even talked Cori into shopping in Texarkana, which is about an hour away. Cori would never have done that before she met Kathy. She never went to Texarkana or any place else without me.

They would sometimes be gone all day on a Saturday or Sunday and exhausted when she got home. Kathy taught Cori some new card games, and we played them when we all got together. I could tell Cori loved the unique friendship we were developing with the Tuttles. Cori had a new spark, and her face lit up when discussing them. It was good because I was busy working, just trying my best to catch the "bad guys."

After our BBQ with Bruce and Kathy the following week, I asked Cori what she thought about me taking Bruce fishing on Saturday. I said, "Why don't I take him fishing, and after we catch a mess of fish, we'll have a good old-fashioned fish fry." She thought it would be a great idea, so I called Bruce and asked him if he would be interested. He said he would love to but didn't have any fishing gear. I told him not to worry about it; I had everything he needed.

I told him I would pick him up at about 6:30 on Saturday and ensure he wore jeans and boots. He knew about the snakes in Arkansas but didn't know how dangerous they were where we fished. I told him we have six poisonous snakes in our area, Coral Snake, Timber

Rattlesnake, Pigmy Rattlesnake, Western Diamondback Rattlesnake, Copperhead, and the Cottonmouth/Water Moccasin. Any of them could kill you with one bite if you didn't get to the doctor in time. I explained to him that they could be down by the river, where we'll be fishing, or along a trail on the way to the river. I told him it's hard for them to bite through leather boots, so I told him it would be better to wear them if he had them.

I went by the store on Friday afternoon and picked up our bait. When we got to my favorite fishing hole on Saturday morning, I took a few minutes and showed him how to put on the hook, sinker, and worm. Then, I led him on how to cast the line. At first, he had a little trouble, but it didn't take him long, and he was throwing his line right where he needed it to be. When he got his first fish hooked, he was so excited he didn't know what to do. He forgot he had to start reeling it in. He finally got the hang of it, and after he caught about 5 or 6 fish, he settled down and acted like he had been fishing his entire life. Watching how excited he was to catch those fish and how much he enjoyed it was fun. He acted just like a kid.

We took the fish home and cleaned them, and then he went home to shower so he wouldn't smell like fish when he and Kathy came over. His girls said they didn't like the taste of the fish and decided to stay home. Cori took the fish, rolled them in a flour and cornmeal batter, and cooked them in a big frying pan. They were delicious. Bruce said he didn't think he had ever tasted fish so good. I know he liked Cori's cooking but also bragged about the fish he caught. Kathy and I just laughed and agreed with him. I felt pretty good about teaching him how to catch the fish.

After dinner, we sat around, had a few drinks, and talked for a few more hours. We found out they didn't mind smoking a little pot occasionally, just like Cori and me. I brought out a joint and lit it up, and each of us took turns taking significant drags on it and passing it around until it was only long enough to hold with a pair of tweezers.

We all laughed and enjoyed each other's company when we finished the joint. We finally said good night to Bruce and Kathy at about midnight. It was a lovely day, especially after Bruce learned to catch fish.

Before we left, I told him that he could borrow anything from us if he ever wanted to teach Kathy and his girls how to fish. Kathy looked at me and didn't say anything. She just raised an eyebrow, and when she did that, I knew she and the girls wouldn't be trying their luck at fishing any time soon.

After several months of hanging out together, I asked Bruce if he wanted to learn how to kill and clean a deer. He said he would love to go out and try his luck at it but didn't think he had the stomach to gut and clean one. He said he knew one thing for sure: he couldn't bring it back to his place and clean it. The girls would probably shoot HIM if they knew he killed "Bambi." I got a good laugh but knew many people felt the same way. To me, deer meat was just like eating beef, but it does have a wild taste, and you must get used to it. It's delicious once you acquire the taste. Killing a few deer yearly saved us a lot of money on meat.

I asked him if he owned any guns, and he said he had a couple of handguns but no rifles. I told him I would let him borrow one of mine when we went hunting. I always kept an extra rifle Jason occasionally used in my gun case.

I knew where the deer crossings were up in *t*he woods. I had set up a few deer blinds a few years earlier to go to that location and get a deer just about every time I went out. Most of the time, I hunted out of season, so I didn't care if it was a doe or a buck I brought home. Since it would be his first time, I told him we'd make sure it was a buck.

Before we went for a deer, I had to take him to a place to test his skill with a rifle. I took him to a spot where I always went to try a gun. I set targets about fifty yards away and had him take some shots. At first, he wasn't excellent, and I could tell he'd never fired anything like one of these big guns.

After a few weekends of target practice, we were ready for his big day. We made arrangements with our wives and decided to go out one Saturday morning before daylight. We hiked back up to the deer blinds and set everything up. Most deer don't move around until after daybreak or before dark. That's when they like to feed. I told Bruce we would stay out until he had gotten his deer. We let several days go by before we saw our first buck. When the young buck came slowly strolling down the path toward us, I looked over at Bruce, who was shaking like a leaf on a tree.

I whispered to him to relax and take a deep breath. I told him to take dead aim like he had done with the targets. When the buck got within forty yards of us, I told him to shoot it. When the bullet hit the deer, it buckled and fell on its front knees. It let out a cry, and I told Bruce to reshoot it. On the second shot, it went down for good. I pat him on the back and said, "That was a good shot. You got your first deer." We went to the deer, and I took it and strung it up in a nearby tree by its heels.

I cut its throat and let the blood drain out of its body, just like I had seen with the goat when I was a kid. I cut out its intestines and put them in a gunny sack I had brought because I didn't want to leave anything in the woods. The buck wasn't significant. It only weighed about one hundred pounds. I cut it into two sections, one for Bruce to carry on his back and another for me to carry. Once we hiked back out of the woods with the deer, we threw it and the gunny sack in the back of the truck and headed back home. Bruce was excited about getting his first deer. He talked about it all the way home.

We returned to the house, and I threw the gunny sack in the garbage and took the deer into the garage, where I had a table set up to skin it and cut the meat into pieces like steak. Cori saw that we were back and came running out, all excited. She said, "Did you get one?"

Bruce smiled and said, "Yes, ma'am, I got my first deer." She was very excited and happy for him. *I thought she was a little too pleased about it, in my opinion.*

Teaching him how to kill the deer was like what I had gone through with Jason when he was ten. Jason's reaction was very similar to Bruce's. I asked Bruce if he wanted to take some meat home with him. He scratched his head as he thought about it momentarily and said that he didn't know it would be a good idea. Before he did anything else, he just wanted to get Kathy used to him killing a deer. I told Bruce we would have deer meat at our next BBQ and see how he liked it. He thought that was a great idea.

About two weeks later, I decided to take Mr. Callahan up on his offer to go coon hunting with him. I went to his place to talk to him about it, and I received the same familiar greeting, but when he recognized me, he put down his gun and motioned for me to come up to the porch. I could see the apprehension in his eyes. He probably thought, what the hell did my boys do now? I immediately told him this was not about the boys. It was a social call. His demeanor instantly changed, and he became the same friendly guy when I left his place. I told him that I wanted to ask him a favor. He looked me apprehensively in the eye with his cold stare and said, "What is it?"

I replied, "I have a new friend who moved down the road. He would be what we all call a city slicker. I said, "He's a nice guy but hasn't seen much about how country folks like us live."

He said, "You mean he's like Mayor Stonewall?"

We laughed as I said, "Yeah, just like him." I told him I had taught Bruce how to fish and hunt deer, but I wanted to take him on a "coon" hunt. I asked him if it would be possible if Bruce and I could join him on his next hunt. I told him that I didn't want to keep any of the raccoons; I just wanted Bruce to see how hunting and tree them with the dogs. He got excited and said, "Why don't we just plan a day and time right now?" We set a time to meet him the following Friday at

5:00 pm. He said, "Be ready to hunt all night because once we leave here, we don't return till morning."

I asked him if there was anything we needed to bring.

He said, "No, just bring your feet because we'll be walking all night." As I was leaving, I told him I wouldn't return to see him until Friday, so I expected us to be there. He said, "We'll be waiting."

I could hardly wait to get home from work that night as I went by Bruce's house to tell him I had set up a date and time to hunt with Mr. Callahan. He checked with Kathy to ensure that the date was okay with her. She said, "Sure, Cori, the girls, and I will find something to do that night." Kathy asked if we would bring one of those dead critters home, and I told her no.

I replied, "We're just going for the fun."

She wrinkled up her nose as she turned her back and started doing something else, whispering sarcastically, "Ooooh, so much fun."

Some women don't understand the excitement guys get from doing that. I told Bruce that we didn't have to bring anything but made sure he wore his boots, jeans, long-sleeved shirt, and coat. I could tell that he was very excited.

I asked Jason if he wanted to go with us the following week, but he said he had plans to do something else on Friday night at the school. They were having a football game or something, and he wanted to go. I could tell he was starting to get interested in the girls, and I was a little relieved he didn't want to go because I didn't tell Mr. Callahan that the three of us might be going.

Bruce and I rode in my truck on the way up to Mr. Callahan's place. We were both excited. We discussed things guys talk about when they're away from their wives. We discussed each other's wives, kids, families, and backgrounds. We talked about other women we had been with, but that wasn't many for him since he married Kathy right out of high school. We were becoming excellent friends, and I was starting to like and trust him.

We finally got to Mr. Callahan's; his truck was out front, and two dogs were in the back. They seemed excited about going on the hunt because they went back and forth inside the truck's bed. They were barking like crazy. You could tell they couldn't wait to get started. Mr. Callahan was happy to see us and came over and shook Bruce's hand as I introduced them. He said, "We hunt with oil lanterns for light. I'll give each one of you to carry once we get started. We'll be driving about ten miles deeper up in the woods. I'm not particularly eager to hunt close to home because the dogs would take off during the day and hunt alone, and we may lose them. Then we'd have to hunt them down and bring them back." That made sense to me.

He handed us each a gunny sack and said, "Hang on to these in case we get a couple of those rascals."

He stopped momentarily, looked at me, and asked me if we wanted a shot of moonshine before we took off. Bruce had probably never tasted moonshine before, so I willingly said, "Sure, but just a swallow for me." I couldn't wait for Bruce to try it. I was snickering when Mr. Callahan handed us each a glass. I quickly gulped mine down like soda pop and looked over at Bruce. He was watching me and followed my move. After he swallowed his drink in one large gulp, he immediately stuck out his tongue and let out a yell as if someone had just punched him in the gut. I couldn't help it by then. I was dying laughing. As he laughed at Bruce, Mr. Callahan got a kick out of it.

Bruce looked over at me and said, "Thanks a lot; you're an asshole."

I was still laughing as I said, "What did I do? You're the one who swallowed the stuff.

Mr. Callahan got a couple of rifles for one of his boys, and we took off. Since there were four of us, we took two vehicles. Bruce and I followed him and his son as we drove deep into the woods. Bruce was still talking about the moonshine when we arrived at our hunting location. It was dark by the time we got there. Mr. Callahan lit the oil lamps and handed each of us one. He also had one he would carry and a flashlight that he stuck in his back pocket.

We grabbed the gunny sacks, and they grabbed their rifles, and then he turned the dogs loose. As soon as they jumped out of the pick-up, they started barking and sniffing around. It didn't take long before they got a raccoon scent and took off baying as they ran deeper into the woods. Before we knew it, they were about a half-mile away, and you could still hear them baying as they were hot on the trail of one of them. Mr. Callahan said, "Come on, boys, we got to catch up." We first took off in a bit of jog until we got closer to the dogs. It seemed like we had walked for over an hour until Mr. Callahan said, "Stop," We all stopped walking and listened for the dogs. He said, "They have one treed." He could tell just by the sound of the dog's bark. Their barking changed once they had one tree. They were off in the distance, and catching up with where they were took another thirty minutes.

When we got to the dogs, they were under a large tree, going around and around the trunk, occasionally jumping up on it, and making that half-bark and half-howling sound when they've trapped an animal. Mr. Callahan took out his flashlight and shined it up in the tree. Sure, enough, there was a coon way up, high in the tree. He asked Bruce if he would like to shoot it down. Bruce was more than excited to try it. He took a couple of shots at it and finally killed it, and it dropped. The hounds were all over it as it hit the ground. Mr. Callahan gave them a verbal command, and they immediately backed away. We had just bagged our first "raccoon." Bruce was on cloud nine, and I must admit, I was excited too. I forgot how much I enjoyed doing those hunts.

It didn't take long, and the dogs picked up another scent, and we were off to the races again. As we ran to catch up with the dogs, I almost fell into a big round hole in the trail. It was about eight feet in diameter and about thirty feet deep. Mr. Callahan grabbed me just before I fell in. We took his flashlight and looked over its edge to the bottom.

It had water in the bottom, and a couple of copperhead snakes were swimming around. I asked Mr. Callahan what it was, and he said it was an old, abandoned uranium mine. He said they had them throughout the hills in Arkansas. You must be careful, or someone could fall into one just like you almost did. He said, "That's just one reason we never hunt alone." I was very thankful that I didn't fall in. If I didn't die from the fall, the snakes would've bitten me, and I would probably die before they could get me to the hospital.

After about another hour, the dogs had another one treed. This time, Mr. Callahan let me shoot it out of the tree. We got three that night when Mr. Callahan asked, "Have you boys had enough?" Those were happy words to my ears. I felt like we had already walked about twenty miles through those hills. I looked at Bruce and could tell he was ready to head home, too. Now, the big question I was thinking about is, *how do we find our way back to the trucks?* Mr. Callahan's son had the dogs on a leash so they wouldn't take off after another coon.

Mr. Callahan seemed to know what I was thinking as he said, "Don't worry, boys, I have been hunting up in these woods all my life. I know exactly where we are. We'll be back at the trucks in about an hour." I was happy to hear that because I was tired and anxious to return to the trucks. It was about an hour before dawn when we finally got back. We both thanked Mr. Callahan and his son for the successful hunt and the moonshine and were soon on our way home.

We were still high from shooting those Racoons out of the trees. The only thing on our minds was getting back home and catching up on our sleep. I dropped Bruce off at his house and headed home. After several hours of sleep, Bruce called our house. He first talked to Cori and told her how much fun he had. I got on the phone, and Bruce thanked me for taking him on the hunt. He said it was one of those "once in a lifetime" experiences for him and that he enjoyed it and would never forget it. I told him that he was welcome and that maybe we would get a chance to do it again sometime.

Everything we did from then on seemed to be with Bruce and his family. Bruce and I spent much of our spare time hunting or fishing. We also spent much time with our families, having dinners and playing cards.

Jason had also formed an excellent friendship with Ashley and Stephanie. When we got together as a family, they always went into the other room to watch TV or just hung out together. Jason was almost fifteen then, and when I wasn't doing something with Bruce, I was teaching Jason how to drive. It was easy because we didn't have much traffic on the dirt roads where we lived. It didn't take him long, and he drove like a pro. I couldn't help but think *I wished I would've been able to do that with Spencer and Travis, but that was another time and another world to me.* I hadn't seen Travis for a few years, but I talked to him occasionally on the phone.

When I asked Jason what vehicle he would like to drive to school, he said he would like an older model pick-up. I knew he was like me and preferred the black pick-up. I talked to Cori about it, and we kept our eyes open to see if we could get one for him.

I got a call from the mayor of our little town, and he said he would be retiring soon and would put my name in for the nomination of the town mayor. I told him thanks, but no thanks. I didn't need that kind of attention, so I told him I didn't want the mayor's job. He said he thought I would be perfect for the job. I was thinking *if he only knew about some of the things I'd done, they would've put me in jail and thrown away the key.*

A few days later, I got a call from Bruce, and he jokingly said, "It's a good thing you didn't run for mayor. You would've had keys to the city. We would've all been in trouble then. I wouldn't have known what to call you, Sherriff, or Mayor. I would've just called you "MayShiff." Then he started laughing like crazy. He wasn't the only one who thought the whole thing was a big joke. Cori and I laughed about it for days. Jason started calling me Mr. Mayor for a while instead of dad and would crack up every time he said it. That lasted for about a month before everyone had their laughs.

***

Chapter 15 - Working with Bruce

A few months passed, and a job came up for a Deputy Sherriff in our County. When the opening was official, I immediately went to Bruce and Kathy's house and told Bruce about it. I knew he didn't have any law enforcement training, but I figured I could spend some time and help train him, just like I taught him how to fish and hunt. The pay wasn't as much as I was making, but I figured that with the money Bruce had put away from his severance pay, and that he didn't have a mortgage payment, they could live well on the salary.

I told him he would drive a county deputy Sherriff's car with the gas, maintenance, and meals included. Even though Bruce was a city employee at Hot Springs before moving to Broken Arrow, he was still a little apprehensive about taking the job. I told him that jobs like that didn't occur in our area very often and that he should consider taking it. I told him I'd use my influence to see if they would hire him, and then I would take some time to let him ride with me for a few months, at least until he got used to everything.

Bruce and Kathy wanted to discuss it, and I understood that because I talked over everything with Cori before I made a commitment that involved her or my job. When I got home, Cori was talking to Bruce on the phone, and she seemed excited. She said that he had called, wanting to speak to me. When I got on the phone with him, he told me that he and Kathy talked it over, and they thought it would be an excellent job for him.

Bruce went to the office the next day and applied for the job. After a week or so, he got the job. He called to let me know and thanked me for thinking of him. I said, "You're my best friend and the one I thought of first. There isn't anyone else with which I would rather work." He asked me if I knew when he would start to work, and I told him that he had to go through all the formalities one would have to go through. It would be the same as I did when I got the job. They would have him go to the county office within the next few days and swear him in. I said, "You'll be part of the law enforcement world."

You could tell in his voice that he was excited yet apprehensive about what lay ahead. Now, he would be my best friend, who I hung out with on the weekends and during work hours.

After getting him trained, I knew he would have to cover all parts of the county, just like the other deputy. He would be only one of the two Deputies under my supervision. We already had Bobby Goldsmith in our office with the Sherriff's department for a few years.

When Bruce finally came to work, I spent a few days getting him used to the office and the staff. I showed him where the holding cells were, the evidence room, and his desk to use. The office assistant was very excited to hand him the keys to his car, and he was assigned a pistol, shotgun, and a Billy club.

Once he had everything, I started taking him out to get used to the different towns we covered. In the first month or so, we drove around a lot. We pulled over speedsters, answered domestic disturbances, and went out and checked on illegal pot-growing areas. I showed him how to keep peace with the people by warning them that they just needed signs and tickets from those who needed them. I led him to keep himself out of a tight situation if someone tried to kill him for pulling them over. I told him he had to be careful about something as minor as an argument over what someone thought was a "bogus stop or arrest." He picked up things fast, so training went quickly.

A significant problem in our county was a country and western bar in one of our towns called "The Dump House." We had helped the local police take care of a huge fight that had broken out or picked up someone drunk and disorderly. I found out a long time ago that anytime you have alcohol and women together in a bar with many young guys, you're going to have some problems. Most of the time,

I would call the local police and let their departments handle the situation.

The bar was always dark, even during the day, but I liked that about it. It had four pool tables and a large dance floor, and the bar wrapped around it in an "L" shape. It had bar stools that held approximately thirty people at a time. I told Bruce that I liked to go to the bar sometimes, and after I was done with my day, I would have a drink or two and relax. I asked Bruce if he wanted to go check it out sometime. He said, "Sure, anytime."

A few weeks later, we had driven around all day, and it was about 5:00 in the afternoon. We were both tired of driving, so I took him to the "Dump House" bar. When I walked in, the bartender waved and yelled, "Hey, Cody." I said, hey, back to him as I walked up and asked him how he was doing. I then introduced Bruce to him.

I told him that Bruce was a new deputy and that he would be coming by from time to time to call Bruce if they had any trouble. He asked me if we were going to have a drink. I said, "Yes, my usual good old Jack and Coke." Bruce told him he would have the same. We took a couple of stools at the end of the bar, back where it was a little darker and away from the main floor.

We'd only been there a few minutes when a few servers came over and said hello. They asked how things were going with me. I said things were good, and I introduced them to Bruce. After talking to us for a few minutes, they served drinks to the other customers.

After Bruce and I had our first drink, I asked him if he wanted to shoot a game of pool. We grabbed a couple of pool sticks and flipped a coin to see who would break. We were in the middle of our second game when a young dark-haired girl I had met there before came slowly inching up close to me. She wasn't paying any attention to Bruce as she nuzzled against me. It was wintertime, and she wore the short cut-off, tight jeans, a tight top, and a zip-up sweater. Her breasts were sticking out of the sweater top, and she looked and acted extremely flirty and sexy.

She had been sitting over in the corner with some friends, and I hadn't noticed her, but she saw me when we first came in. She waited a few minutes to let Bruce and I have time together before she came over to say hello. We stopped our pool game for a few minutes, and I took a little time to talk to her. She whispered in my ear as she unbuttoned my shirt, slid her hand inside, and rubbed my chest, "Would you like to go outside and take care of me, Cody?" I was a little embarrassed that Bruce saw what she was doing. I'd never told him that I'd ever cheated on Cori.

I quickly dismissed her and said, "Hey, Stacey, this is our new deputy, Bruce Tuttle." I looked at Bruce, and I could tell he was shocked by how he looked at me. I pulled her aside and said I couldn't talk to her right now and would return and see her in a few days. She smiled and said, OKAY and then quickly scurried away.

Bruce and I finished our game of pool, returned to the bar, and finished our drinks. I threw some money on the bar for our drinks and a tip, and then we left. We quickly said goodbye to the waitresses on the way out the door. I told the bartender to call me if they had any trouble or if it got too rowdy. He laughed with a knowing smile, "You know I will, Cody."

On the drive home, I could tell Bruce was having problems with what he had seen at the bar. I asked what was bugging him. He said, "Your business is yours, but I was slightly surprised that the young girl was coming onto you as she knew you. I always thought you and Cori were tight with each other and that you wouldn't do something like that. Cori is one of the most beautiful women I've ever met, inside and out. What could make you ever want to cheat on her?"

I told him that the girl didn't mean anything to me. She was just a bar girl. I told him I had sex with her a few times, and that was all. It was only about sex with her and me, and that was it. I told him what

Cori and I have together is unique. IT'S NOT JUST ABOUT SEX. To me, making love to Cori is sensual and almost erotic and is true love.

I asked Bruce, "Haven't you ever had sex with another woman since you've been married to Kathy?" He was somewhat reluctant to tell me but finally admitted that he had.

He said he did, but it was a long time ago when they were first married. He said one of his old high school girlfriends kept after him until he finally broke down and had an affair with her. He said that he and Kathy had gone through some rough times and weren't sure if they wanted to stay together when it happened. He said they even separated for a few months but decided it was too hard on the girls to be apart. He said that he had a few sexual encounters during their marriage with other women, but they didn't mean anything to him, like me. He said, "Kathy can be a little overbearing at times and a little pig-headed, but we try hard to keep our marriage together."

He continued about what a great person he thought Cori was and that it was hard to believe anyone would ever want to cheat on her. He asked me if Cori had ever cheated on me. I said, "If I knew about it, she and the guy wouldn't live to talk about it afterward."

He looked shocked when I said that. He said, "What do you mean?"

I said, "I told Cori when we first got together that it was forever, and if I ever caught her with another man, I would kill them both."

Bruce could tell I was serious about what I was saying because I had a seriously mean and angry-looking snarl on my face as I said it. Just the fact that he asked me that question and thinking about it made me angry.

He said, "But don't you think that's being just a little two-faced since you've had sex with a lot of different girls?

I said, "Yes, I suppose so, but that's how it is." I told him it would be better to let what happened back at the bar and the conversation. We had to go any further than just the two of us. He could tell I wouldn't take much more of this interrogation from him, so we agreed it would be best to keep everything to ourselves. That was what best friends are supposed to do. We never spoke about it or brought up the subject of cheating on our wives again.

One day, we were at the office and got an APB (all-points bulletin) that a couple of guys had robbed a bank in Hot Springs and killed a police officer while fleeing the scene. They put out the bulletin so we would be on alert for an older model white Chevrolet. The guys had gotten away with an undetermined amount of cash and headed out of town. The Hot Springs police department didn't know where they would be heading but told us to watch for a suspicious vehicle with two white males.

They also said to be careful because they were armed and dangerous. It became personal for me and everyone in the law enforcement field. I told Bruce to jump in my squad car, and we would go out and patrol some of the roads and see if we could spot them. I told Bruce we could stop them if they came through our area. We didn't think they'd head up our way because of the large number of potholes in the dirt roads and the winding roads up in the hills in our area.

The police department secured the roads in Queensland, and we headed up on highway 71, which headed north. We set up a stakeout a few miles out of town and on the side of the road. We waited to see if they crossed through in the vehicle. We stayed a few hours, and then we saw what we thought might be the suspects' car as they passed by us at a high rate of speed.

I threw on the flashers and pulled behind them to see what they would do. The idiots took the bait and took off at a high rate of speed. Their car climbed in speed and soon exceeded one hundred miles per hour as they tried to outrun us. It wasn't their lucky day, as we stayed right behind them. Bruce called on the radio to say we were in hot pursuit of the suspects.

I pulled my car up as close to them as possible without hitting them, trying to get a good look at them to see if they were the two guys. That's when the guy on the passenger side stuck out his head and shoulders and fired a couple of shots at us. I momentarily backed off to where we were about forty yards behind them. I told Bruce we would end their "Bonnie and Clyde" joy ride. I told him we weren't going to wait for backup. I said, "They had just shot at the wrong guys."

I told him that I knew about a deep ravine about a mile or so up the road on the right and that I would run them off the road straight into that ravine.

Bruce was scared, and he said, "You're crazy! You'll get us both killed." By then, my adrenaline was pumping. I was high on adrenaline, just like I had been before when I got rid of a few other scum bags. I held back a little until we reached the marker, indicating the ravine was coming up. I sped up to where my right bumper was just about touching their left bumper.

The passenger was getting ready to take another few shots at us when I floored the gas and rammed their car hard in the left corner. By then, we were both going over one hundred miles per hour. When I hit them, our car started to weave back and forth, and I fought to control it as I slowed down. Their vehicle turned sideways and went flying off the road. It flipped several times as it did a swan dive and landed on its roof in the ravine.

Bruce was hanging on for dear life as we came to a stop. I backed up my vehicle to where they went off the road, and we both jumped out of the car with our weapons drawn. Dust was still flying as we made our way down to the vehicle. When we got there, the car looked like a pancake from the flips it made and landed on its roof. The guys looked like they were dead, from what we could see. They were going at speed, and the car's shape didn't think anyone could've survived the plunge. There was no way to get them out of the vehicle, so we just returned to our patrol car and waited. Bruce was sitting there, white as a ghost.

I was a little surprised he didn't wet his pants. I could tell that was the scariest thing he had ever gone through in his life. I thought this big, tough-looking guy was just a pussy. Bruce finally realized that I was not only the ordinary guy next door and that he saw that I had just crazy enough in me to make me dangerous.

We got on the radio and called to inform everyone that the guys were on highway 71. We told them we had rammed their vehicle when they shot us at the bottom of a ravine. It didn't look like anyone survived. I called for the coroner.

We waited about ten minutes until backup arrived. We soon had Police and Sherriff cars at the scene. It was important for our county. Everyone was happy that those guys were no longer threatening anyone else.

When we returned to the office, everyone was clapping for us and saying, "Way to go, guys." It was the first time I could make a big deal out of killing someone. Sure, I was glad to get these two thugs off the street, but more importantly, they got what they deserved for shooting at us and killing the police officer.

The following week, I turned Bruce loose, and he was alone. He didn't have me to "babysit" him anymore.

***

Chapter 16 – Cori's changing

It wasn't too long after killing the two thieves when Bruce's attitude toward me started changing toward us. We were still friends with him and Kathy, but we no longer spent all our spare time with them. I thought it might have been because I was running the two guys off the road, and Bruce thought I was a little crazy. After that, I figured he didn't want to be around me as much. I scared him, and he realized I had a dark side of me, and he was a little afraid of that.

Something was happening with Cori at that time. She dyed her hair to its original color to remove a few grey areas and lost a little weight. She was wearing tight jeans again. I thought she looked sexier than I had seen her long ago. I kept telling her how good she looked and had difficulty keeping my hands off her.

The hours at her work had changed, and she was now working from 4:00 pm to midnight, five days a week. I didn't like her working that shift because I only saw her long after midnight and on the weekends. She would get up early in the morning, catch me off to work and Jason off to school, then go back to bed until she had to get up and get ready for work.

Our relationship was starting to become a little strained. For the first time since we had been together, Cori began not going along with what I wanted or asked to do for me. She became agitated if I said something she didn't like. Our sex life was diminishing to the point where she would get frustrated at me for touching.

It seemed to me as though she was spending as little time alone with me as possible. I tried to talk to her about it, but all she would say was, "Everything is fine with me, Cody. Just leave me alone, and I'll be fine." I remember feeling a little suspicious that something else was happening with her, but I didn't accuse her of anything.

Like most guys, when things are wrong with their wives or girlfriends, all I wanted to do was try and fix it. The harder I tried, the worse things got. It seemed like I was kissing her to make things better. Nothing was working, and I was becoming increasingly frustrated with our relationship.

I told her I thought she should quit her job and stay home, and she got angry when I suggested that. She said she loved her job and wasn't going to stop. For the first time since we'd been together, she refused to do something I asked of her.

I tried to get her to take some time off work and leave with me for a few days out of town. She told me she didn't think that was a good idea either. There was nothing I could do or say to make things better. I finally started developing the attitude, to hell with it. There's nothing I can do to make her happy right now, so I'll leave her alone.

I started spending more time at the "Dump House" bar every chance I got. I knew that Jason was with his friends at school, Cori was at work until midnight, and I didn't want to come home to the lonely four gray walls closing in on me.

The more I was alone, the more my mind started to play tricks on me. I started thinking about all kinds of things about Cori. I started believing she had a boyfriend from work, which was why she pushed me away. I started asking people we knew if they noticed anything happening with her. No one seemed to know anything about Cori or her personal life. They sure didn't know about her having a boyfriend from work or elsewhere. I talked to the girl from work who used to pick her up and take her home. She told me that Cori spent much time on the phone with someone during her breaks. She didn't know who it was but assumed it was me because she said Cori was always happy after getting off the phone.

I waited a few days until the weekend, sat down with Cori, and confronted her about how she had been treating me. I asked her about the person she'd been talking to on her breaks at work. She said she spoke to Kathy on the phone during the few minutes she was not working. That made sense because they were good friends with a lot to say. I was starting to think that the suspicions in my head were figments of my imagination.

The darkness was creeping in, trying to take over my brain and make me believe things I thought were true. I depressed those feelings and decided to ride it out just as Cori suggested. She told me things would improve with time and that we shouldn't push it. I still didn't know what she discussed, but I let it do my work.

When I got a call from my mom saying that her brother, Buddy, had died of a heart attack in California, all my thoughts and memories came rushing back about the good and bad times I had spent with him. My mom wanted to know if I would drive her to California to go to the funeral together.

I talked to Cori about what happened, and she thought it would be good for me to go to the funeral.

I was still apprehensive about our relationship and leaving her, but I decided to go. I made arrangements with work, called my mom back, and told her I would pick her up the following day and head to California.

The thought of being with my mom for several days was working on my brain. I wasn't sure how I was going to get through it. I was hoping I didn't lose it with her and must kill her and dispose of her body somewhere along the way. I know it was just crazy thoughts, but you think of things like that, especially when you're with someone pushing your buttons and having a love/hate relationship.

When I picked my mom up, she cried over her brother's loss for a few days. She made me feel sorry for her for the first time. I tried to comfort her by telling her that everything would be okay.

On the way to California, I told her about some of Buddy's fun times with no one else I knew anything about except Buddy and me. I had her laughing a few times about what we did. She also told me stories about him when he was a kid. I wasn't interested in them because I only knew the Buddy I saw when he was growing up. I listened to her just the same. I told her he wasn't the nice guy you and everyone else thought he was. I told her about some dark things he and I had done. I tried my best to be sympathetic to her and give her the support she needed.

We got to California after about a day and a half of driving. I tried to go straight through without much rest. Cori had already been trying to reach my aunt in California to see if I had gotten there safely. That seemed strange because she hadn't talked to my aunt in several years. Plus, she had never done that with any other trips I had taken to California. I used my aunt's phone and called her back to ease her mind. I told her that we arrived safe, that I loved her, and would call her later that evening. She said she loved me too and was happy we got there safely.

The next day, we went to the funeral home and viewed Buddy's body and then spent some time saying our goodbyes to his stiff and well-groomed body. I spent some time alone with his body and told him he didn't have to worry about anything anymore. I told him, "Maybe we'll meet again someday in that place in the sky." I wasn't sure if I meant heaven or hell, but I was sure there would be a place where we would probably see each other again.

That evening, I got another call from Cori saying she was checking up on me to see how I was doing. She said she knew how close I had been to Buddy during my life and wanted to make sure I was doing all right. I told her everything was fine, and everyone was shocked that he had died so suddenly at such a young age. We talked for a few minutes, and I told her I would stay a few more days to let my mom have some time with her other brothers and sisters before we headed back.

I told her I wanted to visit some of my cousins and catch up on their lives. I tried to find out what they had been doing for several years. Some of my cousins owned their businesses and were doing well financially. I wanted to renew some of the bonds we had built when we were younger, and it would be good to see them. I also wanted to spend at least one day with Travis before we left.

Cori called every morning and night for the next four days I was there. It bothered me a little that she gave me more attention now than when I was home.

After we buried Buddy, I spent time with Travis, my cousins, and Aunts and Uncles over the next few days.

We decided to head back to Arkansas after being gone for about a week. I called Cori on the phone before we left and told her we would be home in about 36 hours. I told her I would drive straight through and stop taking a short nap someplace before dropping my mom off.

It was good that my mom was with me because some bizarre things were going through my mind on the way back about Cori. *Why did Cori keep calling me every night and every morning to ensure everything was okay with me? Why was it so crucial for her to know where I was?* I was becoming very suspicious of her. I even talked to my mom about some of my suspicions. She wasn't much help and told me it was all in my head.

My mom was like a sad little chatterbox back in Arkansas, and I was finally glad to drop her off. Mom told me she loved me and hoped she didn't lose me like she lost Buddy while still young. I told her I would be fine and not to worry about me. I laughed as I said, "You couldn't kill me back when I was a kid from the beatings. I'll survive this old world now." She didn't think that was very funny, but it was my way of letting her know that I wasn't happy with the beatings she gave me as a child. I got home, Cori was at work, and Jason was at school, so I just went to bed to catch up on some much-needed sleep.

***

Chapter 17 - Jason's Truck

Jason was turning sixteen soon, and since he wanted to drive a pick-up to school, we decided to look around and see if we could find a classic model 1953 Ford. That one was my favorite of the old trucks, but was also hard to find. I had been looking for one for a few months and made inquiries throughout the state. I finally got a call from an older woman in Little Rock. She told me that her husband had just died, and he had one of those old trucks in their barn and hadn't driven it for years. I asked her if it would start up, and she said, "Your guess is as good as mine, Sonny."

On one of the days I was supposed to be working, I decided to drive up to Little Rock and look at it when I got to the older woman's house (she lived in town but had an old barn behind her house). She was waiting for me when I arrived in her rocking chair on her porch. This old gal was in her eighties and had stories to tell. She was anxious to say them to someone. She told me all about how her husband had repurchased the brand-new pick-up when it first came out at the car dealership. She said he drove it around town for years, but that was about it. He never took it on long trips, so it had few miles.

When we opened the doors to the barn, I could tell this was just the pick-up for Jason. It was dark green on the outside, with a black interior. The interior was still in pretty good shape but needed new tires. There weren't any dents, dings, or scratches in the paint visible outside the pick-up. Her husband had taken great care of it. I brought a battery and some cables because I knew it wouldn't start very quickly if it had been sitting for a while.

I drove my patrol car into the barn and hooked up the cables. She gave me the keys and said, "Give it a whirl, Sonny." After the engine cranked over a few times, I finally got it started. I opened the hood and looked at the motor, and it looked almost brand new, except for some severe dust. I asked her how much she would take for it, and she said she would sell it to me for $800. I didn't have to haggle with her over the price because I knew it was a good deal. I gave her $200.00 to hold it for me and told her I would bring my wife back with the rest of the money on the weekend and pick it up. She said that would be fine, and I left.

I told Cori and Jason about the pick-up that night, and she was excited. I decided to pick it up on Saturday afternoon at a paint and body shop in Texarkana because I wanted to have it painted.

We woke early on Saturday morning and drove to the old lady's house. I introduced her to Cori, and they instantly fell in love with each other. While they were talking, Cori paid her the rest of the money for the pick-up, and I went out and aired up the tires and put some fresh gas in it from a 5-gallon can I brought with me. I started the engine and pulled it out to the front of the driveway. I let it run for a few minutes while we said our goodbyes to the old lady.

I thanked her for letting us have it, but she was also happy that we fell in love with it. She knew it was going to be a good home. I told Cori to follow me to the nearest gas station, and I filled up both vehicles with gas. I checked the water in the pick-up, and we were soon on our way back.

We finally made it to the paint and body shop in the late afternoon. The guy looked at it and said, "Nice. What color do you want?" I replied, "We want to paint it shiny jet black." After looking it over, he said he would have it done by the following weekend. I also asked him if he knew where to get nice rims and tires. He said he would line it up for me, and when we came to pick up the truck, he would send me over to the tire and wheel shop.

The following Saturday came around, and Jason, Cori, and I went to get the truck. It was beautiful, and the paint job came out perfectly. We took it to the tire shop and had Jason pick the new rims and tires. By that time, Jason was biting at the bit to drive it. Even though he didn't have his license, I let him operate it once we got close to home, and the entire time, Cori followed close behind. I told him that we could work on the engine together on the weekends if he wanted to change it or do something different.

Before he got his license, he brought all his friends over, and they drove the pick-up around the dirt roads near our house. He was proud of that pick-up, and I was too. I felt like he was a great kid and deserved something he wanted.

Soon, he got his license and drove himself to school and back. I was happy because Cori nor I had to do that anymore. He was starting to show his independence and growing up. Along with that comes the old familiar arguments with your parents. For the most part, I understood what he was going through, but Cori and Jason started to get on each other's nerves. I thought it was because she had difficulty letting go of her little boy.

Cori and Jason's problems kept escalating to the point where their arguments didn't make much sense to me. After watching and putting up with them for a few months, I decided I'd had enough of what was happening between them and stepped in to see if I could help. I told Jason that I wanted to take him deer hunting the following Saturday and that we should have a man-to-man talk about what was happening between them. Maybe he had a girlfriend he liked at school, and she didn't want him. I was unprepared for what he was about to tell me.

We woke early on Saturday morning and headed to our favorite spot in the woods. It wasn't daytime as we set up our position in the deer blind. As the morning sun rose, I started asking Jason to tell me what was happening with him. I want to know why he fought so much with his mom. I told him I would keep it between us; no one else needed to know, not even his mom.

At first, he was apprehensive about telling me what was causing all the problems between him and his mom. I swore to him I wouldn't say a word to anyone about it. He then told me that he thought his mom was doing it. I said, "Yea, I figured that, but what exactly is the problem?"

He started to break down in tears as he choked out the words. "I think something is going on with Mom and Bruce." I was taken aback by what he said. I never expected him to say something like that. I was in total shock when he uttered those words to me. His words shot through me like a bolt of lightning, cutting me like a knife through the heart. I just sat there looking at him for a minute, trying to absorb what he had just told me. I thought *there was no way that could be true. "Not Cori. She would never be interested in another man." And Bruce? He was my best friend; best friends wouldn't do things like that to each other. I had been with Bruce daily and month after month for the past few years. I couldn't believe it would be possible for something like that to be true.*

I thought that maybe Jason just had a wild imagination. I asked him why he believed that. He said, "I have never trusted that guy with mom since we first met him. He's always had his eye on her."

I held Jason in my arms and comforted him; I tried to gather my thoughts and emotions as best I could. The silent rage started inside me as I asked why he felt that way. He said he talked to Ashley and Stephanie about it for a few months, and they also thought it was true. He said that they started to listen in on conversations that Cori and Bruce were having with each other, and it didn't seem like it was still the "Just best friend" type of exchange. They were friendly with each other on the phone. Now I was starting to get angry. I asked him if Kathy knew anything about what was happening, and he said they hadn't told her anything about it and didn't know if she suspected anything.

I composed myself and told Jason that whatever issues Cori and I were having with each other, he didn't need to carry that burden upon himself. I told him I would closely monitor Bruce and Cori to see if anything was happening between them. I told him he didn't need to worry about it. If there were a problem, I would take care of it. When I told him this, my brain began to relate what was happening with Bruce and Cori to how she had treated me for the past several months. I thought that Bruce must've told Cori about the girl at the "The Dump House" bar and about the private conversations we had with each other concerning other women. Things were starting to look more transparent and make more sense to me.

Jason felt better about telling me because he could get it off his chest. I told him I wouldn't let Cori know that we had talked about any of this, and he was very relieved to hear that. I told him he could stop arguing and fighting with his mom. From now on, it was my problem and not his. He agreed that he would try and do that. We didn't get a deer that day, but we got much more out than just killing a deer.

When we got home, we acted like everything was fine, just bummed because we had come home empty-handed. When I first saw Cori, I wanted desperately to confront her and choke the truth out of her about Bruce after we got home. I kept my promise to Jason and didn't say anything to her. The anger was building up in me like a raging river toward a dam. I was dying inside to confront her and ask what was happening between her and Bruce.

Over the next few hours, I spent a lot of time thinking about what Jason told me and the other things that were now starting to make a lot of sense. Now I knew why she had been so short-fused and irritable with me. I decided to talk with Bruce to see what he had to say about it. I decided that if he said he was having an affair with Cori, I would take him up in the woods by Mr. Callahan's place and torture him before I killed him. Maybe even take him to one of the thirty-foot holes, kill him, and dump him in the hole.

The next day, when we were at the office, I asked Bruce to ride with me. I said I wanted to go up into the woods and check on the women kids molested by their father. He said, "That would be great." I was so angry as we were driving that I could hardly speak to him. He could tell that something was bothering me and asked me what was wrong. I didn't tell him that I was ready to kill him.

When we were deep into the woods, I pulled over in a turn-out of the road. I burst inside to hear how he would answer my questions. I was going to ask him. I was hoping he would say the right thing, or he would soon die.

I slowly started asking him how things were going with him and Kathy at home. He said, "Things are good with us. We're just getting things ready for Stephanie to graduate from high school and go on to college."

I said, "You know, you're my best friend, Bruce, and if you're having marriage problems, you can talk to me about them."

He said, "No. Really. Everything is fine with us. It's just the normal things people go through."

That's when I confronted him about the phone conversations with Cori, and I said, "The kids have voiced concerns to me that you and Cori have been spending a lot of time on the phone talking with each other for the past few months." He looked a little surprised as I said that.

Then he replied, "Yes, to be honest with you, she's been talking to me about you and couldn't figure out what was going on with your marriage."

I said, "What do you mean?"

He replied, "She just wanted to know what was going on with you, and I told her everything with you was fine and that you loved her very much."

That didn't make sense, I thought. *Why didn't Cori talk to me about her concerns, and why would they spend so much time talking about it?* I wasn't buying his explanation when I told him I didn't feel comfortable about the two of them having long conversations about me or my marriage. I told him I wanted it to stop. I told him it hurt my feelings and angered me that they talked to each other about it behind my back.

He said, "You're my best friend, Cody. I wouldn't do anything to hurt you or Cori." He said, "If it makes you uncomfortable, I'll stop."

I asked him if he'd said anything to Cori about the private things we'd talked about, and he said no. I told him again that those two talking to each other made me uncomfortable, and I wanted it to end.

I was also angry that Cori had gained enough trust to talk to him about our relationship without discussing it with me first. The two of them were closer than I wanted them to be. I asked him if anything was happening between him and Cori, and he said, "No, I would never do that to you, Cody." I wasn't sure if he was honest with me, but I couldn't kill him based on my suspicions.

I drove around on the dirt road for a while, pretended I couldn't find the house we were looking for, and then headed back to the office. On the way back, I would put a little validity into how I believed Cori, and someone were having an affair with each other. I told Bruce again about how I felt about other guys hitting on Cori.

I started telling him a story about the new guy who worked in one of Queensland's markets. I told him he was a good-looking young guy in his mid to late twenties. On one of those rare occasions when I went shopping with Cori, I was getting something on the other side of the store, and this young clerk started coming on to her. He knew she was married, but that didn't stop him. He didn't think I was with her then, so I walked behind him. When I got close to him, I heard him ask her if she would like to drink with him sometime. She didn't have time to answer him when I touched her on her waist. I didn't say anything to him. I glared at him angrily as Cori politely said, "No, thank you, I'm married. She turned and pointed at Cody and said, this is my husband, Cody." He reached out to shake my hand, but I looked at him angrily.

A few days later, I went by the store and learned from the manager when the clerk got off work. I told the manager it was official business and did not let the clerk know I asked about him. Later that evening, when he came out of the store, I met him just as he started to get into his car. I didn't say anything to him. I punched him in the face several times and knocked him to the ground. Thankfully, he didn't try to fight back or hurt him.

He looked up at me with a surprised look and said, "What the hell is wrong with you? Why did you do that?" That's when I told him I didn't like him flirting with my wife. He didn't say anything because he already knew who and what I was saying.

I said, "If you want to be alive next week, you'll find another job far from Queensland. Don't let me see you around here again, and don't let anyone know I had this conversation with you, or I will find you and kill you. I'll dump your body in the woods where no one will ever find you." After that incident, I never saw him again in the store or any other in Queensland. He was lucky that he got my message, or I would've killed him.

When I told Bruce that story, I hoped he understood how sincere I was about my threats. I told him, "As you can see, I'm not kidding around about killing someone if they are with my wife. I would've killed him if he hadn't done what I told him."

Bruce was a little nervous as he said, "I know how you feel, Cody, and I'm not ready to die." We both laughed, but mine was more of a nervous, angry laugh. That was the end of the conversation about Cori. We made small talk back to the office, and the rage in me started to subside a little. I still wasn't sure if he was telling me the truth, so I decided to keep an eye on him from now on.

I talked to Jason a week later to see if Ashley and Stephanie had heard more conversations between Bruce and Cori. He told me they hadn't noticed anything unusual in the past week. I talked to my friend from Cori's work, and she said that Cori was still talking to someone on the phone during her break, but it wasn't every day, like before. I started to think I was just a little paranoid about Bruce and Cori, so I began relaxing.

***

Chapter 18 – Finding out about Cori

Several days later, I was at the office and got what I thought was an unusual call from Cori. She asked me what my day at work looked like, and I told her that I was busy working up in the county's Northern area and would probably be gone all day. She said she would go shopping in Texarkana and check to see if I wanted to go with her. I told her I couldn't because of my entire work schedule.

After I hung up the phone, I started thinking about it and called her back. I said, "If I must go, I'll take the day off and go with you."

She then started to backpedal. She said, "No, that's ok. You finish your work, and I'll see you after midnight when I get home."

I said, "Are you sure? I can put my stuff off until tomorrow and go with you if you want me to." She was more than insistent that I go ahead and do my job. She was so insistent; it raised a red flag with me. It made me very suspicious that something didn't seem right. After thinking about it for several minutes, I thought it was odd that she called me and asked me to go with her. She'd never done that in all the years we'd been together. "Why was she asking me to take a day off and go with her now?" Then it hit me. She was trying to find out where I was going to be working.

I couldn't get it out of my head that something didn't feel right, so I asked one of the girls in the office where Bruce was working that day, and she said he was working in another part of the county and would be gone all day. My brain was starting to work overtime, and I thought maybe the two would meet each other somewhere. I asked the office girl if I could borrow her car for the day. I told her I would put gas in it before returning and gave her lunch money. I told her that if Cori or Bruce called, not to let them know that I borrowed her car.

I took her car and headed out to my house. When I drove past my driveway, I could see my pick-up was still there. I drove down the road, past my house, and hid in the tree line. I was waiting to see if she was going to leave. After about fifteen minutes, she left the driveway, heading toward Texarkana. I slowly pulled in behind her and kept a safe distance so she wouldn't see me following her. When she got to highway 71, she headed south to Texarkana. I kept following her at a safe distance until she got almost into Texarkana.

The closer I got to Texarkana, the more I thought, what the hell are you doing? Are you nuts? She's just going shopping, as she said. Feeling foolish about not trusting her, I pulled off the road, turned around, and headed back toward the office.

I had gotten only a few miles when I saw Bruce's patrol car coming from the opposite direction toward me and heading into Texarkana. He didn't recognize me because I was in the borrowed car, and I ducked down when he passed. I went up a short distance, immediately turned around, and started to follow him. He was a little easier to follow because of the lights on top of the patrol car. When we reached the central part of Texarkana, many traffic lights and vehicles were on the road. Somehow, I lost sight of his car near a shopping center. I was pretty pumped up and agitated at that point. I knew something was up with him and Cori.

I started driving all around the area and couldn't spot his car. I was getting angrier and more frustrated by the moment that I couldn't find him. Finally, I decided I would go into the shopping center parking lot, and sure enough, as soon as I drove in, I spotted his patrol car. It was there, but he wasn't in it. I started looking for my pick-up, which wasn't in the parking lot. I was a little relieved. I didn't see it, but my mind told me something wasn't right. I looked for them and even went through all the stores looking for either of them. Bruce and Cori disappeared.

I decided to wait in the parking lot near Bruce's car to see what was happening to him. He had no business in Texarkana; he was supposed to work in another town. I knew he had to come back and pick up his car.

I spent the rest of the morning and part of the afternoon just waiting and going crazy. I was so upset I couldn't even think about eating lunch. Tons of scenarios ran wild, like *Did Cori pick him up, and then they took off somewhere together? If he and Cori are together, did they go to lunch? Are they at some hotel or a park somewhere, kissing and having sex?*

My mind was going in circles, and it was starting to consume me. I was full of anger and rage, and my body began to shake at one point. I had to take deep breaths to calm myself down. I could hear my heart beating as I sat there all alone. I knew the truth, and I was hurting so badly inside. I felt like I wished I was dead. The pain was almost more than I could bear.

It was about 2:00 in the afternoon when Bruce came driving up in my pick-up. Cori was sitting next to him. My heart immediately hit the ground. I felt like someone had just kicked me in the stomach. I felt like my biggest fears had come true. I went over and grabbed him by the collar of his shirt. I pulled him out of the seat and through the open window. Before realizing what I was doing, I slammed him on the ground and kicked him in the ribs twice.

Cori had a defiant, "Oh crap, I'm caught" look on her face. She looked like the kid caught with his hand in the cookie jar. The first words out of my mouth were, "What the hell are you two doing together?"

She said, "Cody, stop, stop. It's not what you think." I had a hard time trying to focus on what she was saying; I was so angry.

"We've been out shopping to buy you a birthday present. I knew you wanted a new rifle, but I didn't know what kind, so Bruce met me here and showed me the one you've been wanting." She then pulled this wrapped present from the passenger seat, and I could tell it was the size and shape.

Now, I was beginning to feel like the biggest fool in the world. I was the one that looked like I had made a colossal mistake. Cori asked me what the hell I was doing in Texarkana. She said, "You're supposed to be working up north." I quickly made up a story and told her I was checking out a guy who was a suspect in an armed robbery. I just happened to drive by and saw my truck with the two of you in it.

She said, "You big dummy. Nothing is going on between Bruce and me."

I felt like I had an egg on my face as I said, "I'm sorry for jumping to conclusions." I tried to apologize, but they both were angry with me. Bruce started walking to his patrol car, and as he left, I apologized for kicking him in the ribs. Cori took the truck and headed back home without saying a word to me.

I got in my borrowed car and headed back toward my office. I felt like a dog with its tail between its legs. I drove very slowly on the way back because I was so embarrassed for making a complete fool out of myself. I'd never felt so much like a complete idiot. Back in the office, I agonized over what I had done.

When Cori got home around midnight, I apologized to her repeatedly. I had already called Bruce and apologized to him a couple of times. After kissing up to them the rest of the week, it seemed like they got over it by the weekend.

Cori told me we were having a BBQ at our house on Sunday with Bruce, Kathy, and the girls to celebrate my birthday. She laughed and said I was getting a new rifle for my birthday. I didn't think it was that funny. By that Sunday, everything seemed forgotten, and Bruce and Cori were back in happy spirits with me again. It was almost back to how things had been with Cori and me. We all had a great time together.

After dinner, Cori, Jason, and the girls took in the dishes. Bruce was in the bathroom when Kathy asked me if I was happy with my new rifle. I said, "Yes, I love it, and it's what I've wanted for a long time.

She said, "I know it was so hard to find. It took Cori and me almost all day to track it down for you. We finally had to get it in Texarkana."

I looked up at her in shock. I couldn't believe what she told me; her words surprised me. I looked her in the eyes with a stunned look on my face. I said, "What do you mean? I thought Bruce and Cori picked it up just this past week in Texarkana."

She said, "Heavens no, Cody. We've had it for weeks, just waiting to give it to you for your birthday."

I was trying to comprehend what she told me when I asked again, "Are you sure? Cori said she and Bruce picked it out for me last week."

Kathy said, "I'm sure. We went into Texarkana one Saturday while you were deer hunting and picked it up about four or five weeks ago."

Suddenly, the anger and familiar pain I had felt in Texarkana slammed me in the chest. My whole body visibly shook with rage. I was right the first time; I had caught them together during their affair. One of the worst parts was that they tried to make me look and feel like a fool. Now, I was even angrier! They lied to me and wanted to make me feel like I was the one who had done something wrong. After I kissed both of them all week, I bet they got a good laugh when they talked.

I was beginning to see the game they were playing. I found out what was going on with Cori and Bruce. They were sneaking around to different places, having sex, and just hoping not to get caught.

Kathy could tell I was visibly upset, but I told her not to say anything about our conversation to Cori or Bruce. She agreed.

That night, when we got home, I didn't say anything to Cori about what Kathy had told me. Inside, even though I loved her, I was dying to choke her or crush her head with something. Their secret was killing me inside. It was ripping me apart, and I wanted to do something.

I lay awake after she went to sleep, thinking about the two of them being together and Bruce kissing her and her kissing him. I could only imagine what they were saying and doing with each other. I was dead inside as I lay next to her. I kept wondering what she saw in him that caused her to want to cheat on me. Was it the fact that he was good-looking? Was it his body or the way he dressed? Was it the way he kissed or made love to her? What was it? It was driving me crazy.

After several hours of no sleep, my pain turned into deep-seated hate and rage. I got up in the middle of the night and just sat on the couch, alone and in the dark. I had to figure out what I would do about the little secret they thought they had so cleverly kept from me. I thought they both had a lot of guts sneaking around behind my back, especially when they knew I would kill them if I caught them.

I had warned them repeatedly that I would kill her and the guy she was with if I ever found out she was cheating on me. They had done the wrong thing to me, and now I was going to figure out a way to make them suffer the same deep, agonizing pain I was going through.

The next day, I went to work. I couldn't concentrate, so I went into my office and closed the door. As I sat there, I started planning how to kill them. Maybe I could take Bruce hunting with me, and while we were hunting, I could shoot him in the back of the head and tell everyone it was a hunting accident. Maybe I could set up another "coon" hunting trip with Mr. Callahan, push him into one of the steep ravines, and say he slipped. Maybe I could take him up in the hills and kill him, tie some rocks to him, and throw him in one of those 30-foot-deep abandoned Uranium holes. No one would ever find him or know what happened to him. Maybe I could sneak some explosives out of the evidence room, plant them under his car, blow it up when he got in it, and turn it on. Everyone would think it was some crazy person he had given some ticket for speeding or something. Maybe I could take him fishing, knock him out, and tie him up. I could have a deadly snake bite him several times. Once he was dead, I would untie him. I would tell everyone that he was fishing down the river and couldn't get out in time. I had a lot of different ideas of how I could kill him and get away with it. I just needed to come up with something that made sense.

As for Cori, I could make it look like someone broke into the house to steal things. Maybe she got in the way, so the thieves killed her.

Maybe I could run the pick-up off the road into a tree and then make sure she was dead by bashing her head into the steering wheel. Maybe I could drown her in the bathtub and make it look like an accident, just like Becky, the photographer from the convention in Las Vegas. I had a lot of different ways I could kill her, too. The only problem with all these plans is how it would look if they both turned up dead within a short time. But I wanted to kill them while they were together.

I had to find a way to do that, and from what I had been hearing and seeing, it wouldn't be that hard. If I caught them while they were having sex, I thought I could shoot each of them in the head and then tell the jury that I had temporary insanity and kill them in a jealous rage. Or, maybe I could put a knife in Bruce's hand and say that he tried to attack me, and I shot him several times, and one of the rounds killed Cori by accident. It would look like I killed him in self-defense and her by accident. Maybe the courts would accept that explanation. I had to plan it all out very carefully to get away with it. I had to make enough money to hire a good lawyer to get me off the murder charges once I killed them. That wouldn't be easy because I didn't control the money in our house. Cori took care of the money and all the bills.

***

Chapter 19 - Getting money from my cousin

I decided I needed to go to California and see my cousins and come up with a way to convince them to loan me the money for attorney fees once I killed Cori and Bruce. I couldn't tell them I was planning to kill my wife and her lover, or they would never loan it to me. They understood real estate, so maybe I could tell them I had an excellent investment deal. I wouldn't let Cori know I was going there to get money from them.

A few days later, I told Cori I would visit California to see Travis and my cousins for about six days. She didn't ask me many questions about it, so I figured she was glad to be getting rid of me so she could carry on her love affair with Bruce.

I was on to her and Bruce now, and I was outraged! It took everything I had to keep from saying anything to either of them without killing them. I desperately wanted to kill them both without waiting. I had to get out of there soon, or I would've killed them. None of my plans had a chance to come together. I also needed time to think about precisely what I would do and how I would do it to get away with it.

On the drive to California, something in my head kept saying she's the woman you love. Maybe you could go to her and talk to her about everything. Perhaps you could forgive her and go back to normal. Something else in my head told me to go back and kill them both as soon as possible. All the good times we had shared and the life we had worked so hard to build kept running through my mind.

I kept thinking about how we couldn't keep our hands off each other, how our bodies felt like they were for one another. I thought Cori was mine forever. Then the ugly side of me thought, Yes, right. She's been screwing Bruce for who knows how long. Simultaneously, she was making love with me and pretending everything was okay. I knew that everything would change when I got back from California.

As I drove along, my angry side took over and started thinking about the lies, sneaking around, and hiding that Cori and Bruce had been doing. How many times were Cori and Bruce in the house having a quickie? In the bathroom or laundry room during some of our late nights? They probably laughed at each other and said, "Look at those fools out there. They're clueless that we're having sex right under their noses." It worked well for them because if they got caught, all they had to say was that Bruce dropped by to pick up something *he* or Kathy left at our house during the last BBQ. What angered me and pushed me over the edge was that he pretended to be my best friend while getting into my wife's pants. I loved him, trusted him, and treated him like a brother. I told him I would kill someone for messing around with my wife on more than one occasion. He thought I was bluffing, or maybe he wasn't scared of me. Perhaps his love for her just blinded his judgment.

While on the way to California, I was mentally exhausted from all the different things going through my head. I stopped at that cowboy bar in Albuquerque, New Mexico, where I had broken the guy's kneecaps several years earlier. The way I was feeling, I didn't much care if someone recognized me and had me thrown in jail or if someone beat the hell out of me. I was like a whipped puppy and an emotional wreck.

When I first walked into the bar, I noticed they had a different bartender and new waitresses. I looked around and didn't see the petite blond or her big, sloppy husband, so I figured I was safe. I didn't sit at the bar this time. I had the bartender give me a Jack and Coke, and I found an empty table hidden in a dark corner of the bar. It wasn't too busy and was just what I needed. I hoped a few drinks would relieve the pain and simmering anger about to boil over in me.

After a few drinks, I came up with the idea that picking up a girl to have a one-night stand might make me feel a lot better. I looked around the room and saw a couple of girls sitting alone at another table. I had the waitress send them a drink from me. Soon, one of the girls came over and thanked me for the drink. She wasn't the prettiest girl I had ever been with, but she was friendly and had a good figure. She sat down and asked me where I was from and what I did for a living. The usual things you ask someone.

It wasn't long before she and I kissed, and I asked her if she had someplace we could go. She said, "Since you're a Sheriff, I can trust you to follow me to my house." She said, "You have to promise me you won't use your cuffs on me." We both laughed, and I agreed as we left the bar. I followed her home and spent a few hours having empty sex with her. I thought being with her might help my sad and angry feelings about Cori. When I started to sober up a little, I told her I had to get back on the road. We thanked each other and said goodbye.

Once I was back on the road, I realized I didn't feel better than before stopping at the bar. I thought I had done something that would've made me feel like I was getting even with Bruce and Cori for what they had done to me, but it didn't work. It was just sexual release, and that was all. It didn't give my brain the relief and satisfaction I hoped to accomplish. I was still hurt and angry inside, and as hard as I tried, I couldn't stop dwelling on them. It was eating me up like nothing I had ever experienced before like cancer spreading and consuming me.

I pulled over on the side of the road and parked as I contemplated my demise. I wondered if death would've been better for me than what I was going through. I had my pistol with me and thought maybe everyone would be better off if I killed myself and ended my misery. After much thought, I put the gun under my chin and pulled the trigger.

Then something inside my brain said, go ahead and do it, you coward. You'll give them just what they want, and that's you out of the way. I thought you said you would kill her and the man she was with *w*hen I heard that. It shocked me back to reality enough for me to put the gun down. I exited the car and went into the bathroom to calm myself down for a few minutes. I then went back to my car and took a nap in the car for a few hours before heading on to California.

Once in California, I saw Travis and spent several hours with him. I told him I might not be seeing him for a while. He was okay with that and said, "Well, I guess I'll see you when I see you, Dad." I spent the rest of the night at his house. We talked about many different things that were going on in his life.

I called my two cousins and told them I'd like lunch the next day. They were surprised but happy I called, and we set a time for the following day. During our lunch meeting, I told them I had found a great deal on a property piece and needed $10,000.00 cash to buy it. I told them the property was worth five times what they were selling. I said the guy had to have the money right away, or he would sell it to someone else. I told them that once I had it in my name, I would put my other place up for sale and pay it back as soon as it sold. One of my cousins had a credit line, and he said he would loan me the money but said he had to get it back. We went straight down to his bank from lunch, and he pulled out $10,000.00 cash and gave it to me. Just like that, I had the money I needed for my defense once I killed Bruce and Cori.

I knew I would never repay my cousin, but that was the least of my worries. I felt like it was his fault for trusting and believing me. He was a fool, but I was glad he gave me the money. They didn't know I had planned to kill my wife and her lover as soon as I got home. The cousin who gave me the money said I looked a little down and wanted to know what was wrong. I told him I'd had a few issues with Cori, but that was no big deal, and I would have them worked out soon. We hugged, shook hands, and I said, "I'll see you again soon." I knew I would probably never see him again. After that, I was on my way back to Arkansas.

On the way home, I thought about what I would do to Bruce and Cori. I figured the best plan was to kill them once I caught them together. I liked the story in which Bruce tried to attack me when I saw them together. I shot him in self-defense, and Cori got hit with one of the stray bullets. That story made more sense to me than any of the others. I just needed to be patient and wait for the right time.

***

Chapter 20 - Confronting Cori

When I got home, I pretended to be happy to be home and acted like nothing was wrong. I hid the $10,000.00 in my secret hiding place. I avoided any intimacy with Cori over the next few weeks.

I started following Bruce on some days he was supposed to work to see where he was going. As I suspected, one day, Bruce ended up at my house when I told Cori I would work in an area about two hours from home. I was outraged to see his car in my driveway, but it didn't feel like the right time to kill them.

Once I knew they were together, I decided to drive over to Bruce and Kathy's house to talk to Kathy about things. I wanted to sit down with Kathy, talk with her, and let her know what I had found out was going on with Bruce and Cori. I also wanted to find out everything she knew. Her girls were at school, so she invited me in when I got there. We sat at the kitchen table, and I told her what I knew about Bruce and Cori's affair. I was stunned to hear that she already knew everything that had been going on between them. She said she had known about their romance for a few months and was surprised that I hadn't learned much sooner. She said that she first found out when her girls made her aware of Bruce and Cori's phone calls to each other. I said, "So when you told me about shopping for my gun with Cori, that was no accident. You were letting me know what was going on with them?"

She cried as she said, "Yes, but I wanted you to find out by yourself. I didn't want to be the one to tell you. I know how much you love Cori."

I replied, "I can't believe them. She was your best friend, and he was mine."

She shrugged her shoulders and said, "Sometimes, friends are the ones who often betray you the most. I guess we made it easy for them."

I asked her what she planned to do about her marriage. She told me that she and Bruce had already discussed it and decided that as soon as Ashley finished her senior year, he would have to move out of the house and find his place to live. She said she had already decided what she would do with her marriage, but it would be up to me to decide what I would do with mine. They were going to file for a divorce right after he moved out. She said he'd already moved into the spare bedroom and that they were not sleeping with each other.

I asked Kathy what she thought I should do. She said I needed to sit down and talk with Cori and find out exactly what was happening and what she wanted to do about our relationship. She said, "You'll know better once you talk to her."

We talked and cried for a little while until I had gotten everything I needed to hear from her. When I got up to leave, I told her I would be there for her and the girls.

I was angry, hurt, and confused, but I thought Kathy might be right. Maybe I needed to confront Cori and see her version of the truth. The only problem was that I wasn't sure what I wanted to hear about what she had to say to me. I didn't know if I could keep from killing her if she told me everything that had been happening. I had been through many painful things, but this one hurt me. I had never felt pain like that before.

It was getting close to Christmas, so I decided to wait until a few days after confronting her. We went through the motions of Christmas, but to me, it was just a blur. All I could think about was that Cori wanted to be with someone else, not me. I was thinking back to when Cori started getting upset with me for little things that didn't matter to her.

I tried to remember when she started getting edgy and upset with me, and I should have realized it all started right after hanging out with Bruce and Kathy. I didn't understand, at the time, why she had changed. I thought she was going through some early change in life or something similar. I never even imagined what was going on with her. It was all a giant puzzle to me, but now all the pieces fit into place.

A few days after Christmas, when Jason was visiting some friends, I confronted Cori and asked if she would tell me the truth about her and Bruce. I was trying very hard to control the demon inside me and not let him come out in a rage and kill her.

I sat down with her quietly and calmly asked what was happening with her and Bruce. At first, she acted like she didn't understand my question and what I was asking her. She said, "What? Why? What do you mean, Cody?"

I bit my lip and angrily replied, "I've heard things from different people about the two of you." She asked me who I had heard that from, and I said, "It doesn't matter who told me. I want to know what's going on between the two of you." She wanted to know where I heard my information, so I finally said, "Kathy already knows about you guys, and she's one of the people who told me. Jason, Ashley, and Stephanie know something is happening between you two."

She asked me, "What have you heard?" I said, "I've heard and seen enough to know that you've been sneaking around and seeing each other behind my back. Don't try to lie to me about it. Just tell me what you've been doing with each other."

She finally broke down and said, "You don't want to know, Cody."

I said, "I have a pretty good idea, so why don't you go ahead and fill me in? If you don't tell me, I'll go to Bruce's house and beat it out of him. I'll make him tell me the truth even if I have to torture him or kill him."

After many threats and prodding, she began to break down and tell me that they started as just friends but said the two had an attraction toward each other. She said it started innocently flirting and teasing, and they eventually ended up kissing and hugging to comfort each other. She said when Bruce told her about all the women she had sex with, it changed her. I had shared all of that in private with him. She said he told her about the girl at the "The Dump House" bar. She said it hurt her deeply to hear all those things about me. She said I loved her enough that I would never cheat on her. She said Bruce was there to comfort and help her through it all.

I was outraged, and I thought he sabotaged my marriage with a low-life, no-good, backstabbing prick. He did it all to get in her pants. He should've kept everything to himself like we promised each other. I dismissed what she said about the other women and asked her, "Is there something wrong with me?"

She looked at me, puzzled, and said, "No, there is nothing wrong with you, Cody. It had nothing to do with you. It just happened the way I told you. He met my emotional needs, and you haven't been there for me for a few years now."

I yelled at her as I said, "What the hell does that mean." I thought I'd been meeting all her emotional needs since we had been together.

We fought back and forth for about an hour, and then I asked her something I knew I couldn't deal with the answer. I asked her the dreaded question, but I believed I already knew the answer, too, "How long have you been having sex with Bruce?"

She looked up at me with tears in her eyes. She was afraid and ashamed and reluctantly said, "For about six months, and I'm sorry, Cody."

At that point, I couldn't take it anymore. I slapped Cori across the face as hard as I could. I busted her lip, and it started to bleed. Right then, I knew I had to get out of there, or I would have killed her.

I pulled out a suitcase and told her I was going to California. I needed to think about things for a while. I just needed time to absorb everything she had told me. She held a small hand towel on her lip as she followed me into the bedroom, begging me not to leave.

She said, "I love you, Cody. I'm sorry this all happened. We can work things out. Let's not give up on our marriage."

I said, "Yeah, but apparently, you love someone else, and you've already thrown it away to be with someone who is supposed to be my best friend."

She cried as she said, "He's not your best friend. He has never been."

I was surprised when she said that, and I didn't respond. Maybe she knew something I didn't. Was Bruce pretending to be my friend the entire time so he could get next to her? The mere thought of him being a conniving and manipulative worm made me even angrier. Nothing is left in our marriage I could ever get over or accept again. I knew if I were to pretend everything was okay, it would eat at me and eventually drive me insane. At that point, it wouldn't matter if I forgave her. I knew I would someday snap and kill her and Bruce.

Once I packed my things, I grabbed my guns and told her, "I have to get out of here, or I'll kill you both." She knew what I was saying was true, so she didn't say anything but that she was sorry as I walked out the door. I could tell she feared what I might do to them. She knew what the consequences of her actions meant to me. We'd talked about it ever since we first met.

I was so angry and upset that I could've gone to Bruce's house that instant and killed him right in front of his entire family. I had to get away and think about things before I did something I couldn't take back. I took my suitcase, threw it in the back of the pick-up, and left. I felt like I was in a time warp or another dimension.

I felt like a zombie you would see on television where they are doing things but don't look like they have any control over their actions. It was like I was on autopilot. My thoughts were going in circles, and my heart was devastated. I didn't even know where I was or what I was doing.

I just started driving, and before I knew it, I was across Oklahoma and into Arizona. I'd been going for about 18 hours when I snapped back to some sanity. I suddenly remembered I didn't get the $10,000.00 hidden in the house. The angry side of my brain was telling me to turn around, go back, and get the money. It also said that I wouldn't let them get away with hurting and deceiving me as they had done. I needed to go back and wait until they were together and then kill them just like I had planned. I was hurting so bad inside that I didn't know what to do. The anger kept building, and before I knew it, I had turned around and headed back to Arkansas.

***

Chapter 21 – I can't control myself

I was both emotionally and physically drained as I made my way back to Broken Arrow. I got there at about 2:00 in the afternoon. I drove past my house to see if anyone was home. Unbelievable as it seemed, Bruce's car was in my driveway. I immediately went into a blind rage, grabbed my pistol, and loaded it. I knew she wasn't sorry for anything, and their actions proved it. She didn't want me to kill them for getting caught.

I couldn't believe those two waited until they thought I was in California to continue their little love affair. They were either insane or just plain stupid. They hadn't believed a word. I told them all those times when I told them I would kill her and the person she was with if I ever found out she did something like that.

I was shaking so badly that I could hardly control myself. I made up my mind that this was going to be the case when I confronted Cori and Bruce. I smoked a little pot to try and calm my nerves before I pulled into the driveway. I slowly walked down the driveway to the house, not wanting to see or hear what I feared most. I parked opposite the bedroom. I got out of the pick-up, careful not to make any noise. I pushed the pick-up door shut enough to make sure it didn't close all the way and make a noise.

I slowly walked over to the kitchen window with my pistol in my hand and behind my back. I very carefully looked in. Cori and Bruce weren't in the kitchen. I went to the living room window and peeked in; they weren't there either. There had to be only one place left for them, and that was in MY BEDROOM. I realized there was only one place for them to be, and I had caught them in the act. I carefully peeped through the corner of the window into the main bedroom. There they were, right in front of me and enjoying themselves, just laughing and having sex. She was on top of him with her head tipped back while she laughed at something he said. It instantly made me sick to my stomach. All the tears, apologies, and begging me not to give up on our marriage had been nothing more than an act. She was a lying, conniving, sneaky bitch. That was why they didn't hear me drive up, and they were too busy having fun, thinking I was on my way to California.

My brain couldn't believe or even comprehend what my eyes were seeing. I turned around with my back up against the wall. I slid down the side of the house in pain. I was crying deep inside, but no sound was coming out. The tears were pouring from my eyes and down my face. I sat there for a few minutes to get my thoughts together. Their laughter echoed through my brain like the beating of a loud drum.

Hearing about them and seeing them with my eyes were two different things. In my wildest imagination, I never thought I would catch them having sex. For some reason, I felt it would've been enough to scare her into staying away from Bruce, at least for a little while after I had the confrontation with Cori a few days earlier.

I was in shock as I tried to compose myself and stood up. I bent down, trying to stay below the window, where Cori and Bruce wouldn't see me. I slowly crept to the back door, took my keys, and quietly unlocked it. I slowly made my way to the main bedroom, being careful they didn't hear me.

Once I got to the bedroom, I stood at the doorway. I watched Cori and Bruce for several seconds and then cocked my pistol's trigger and held it in the air. Now that I was this close, watching and hearing them have sex in the same room sent me into an uncontrollable rage. The anger and pain took over my entire body and mind. I was so angry and hurt my whole body was shaking. It was like I had left my body, and someone else was in control. I'd never been in this state of rage before. With the others I'd killed, I was always under control. Now, it seemed like I was watching myself from above, in some corner of the room. At that point, there was nothing I could do to stop myself.

All the thorough planning to ensure their deaths looked like an accident and self-defense went out of the window. Those plans were no longer relevant. I said, "You guys having fun?" as I pointed the pistol toward them.

Cori screamed, "Cody, don't," and immediately jumped out of bed. She said, "I thought you went to California?" All I could see was her nude body, which I cherished and loved so much, standing right in front of me.

She quickly put on her skirt and tried to find her top when I said, "Surprise." She started to come toward me, apologizing. Cori was screaming that she was sorry. I hit her in the head with the butt of the pistol. It knocked her unconscious. Blood was pouring from the spot where I hit her. I looked at Bruce as he started to get out of bed.

He said, "Hey, Cody, wait a minute. Let me explain."

In a deep and uncontrollable voice I was unfamiliar with, I started yelling, "You were supposed to be my best friend. You were supposed to stay away from my wife." When he rose to say he was sorry, I shot right at his head. I tried to kill him, but the bullet grazed his forehead and knocked him unconscious.

I went over to Cori and turned her over on her stomach. I stomped on both legs and broke them right above her ankles. I could hear the crunching of the bone as I stomped each leg. I knew this would stop her from trying to run from me. I then pulled Bruce's limp body out of bed, put his face down on the floor, and stomped both legs right above the ankles, the same as I had done with Cori. I could hear the same crunching sound, so I knew neither was going anywhere. They couldn't walk and would only be able to drag their bodies with their elbows. I had them right where I wanted them, helpless like a wounded deer.

Soon, Cori woke up, screaming in pain from her broken legs. I told her to shut up, or I would put a bullet in her head. She saw the rage in my eyes, and with one look at my face, she knew that I'd lost all control. She was whimpering in pain and started pleading with me not to kill her. In a calm and quiet voice, I squatted beside her and said, "I warned you not to cheat on me." I told her I would kill both, but I would make them both suffer before I killed them, just like they had made me suffer.

A few minutes later, Bruce woke up, yelling in pain from his broken legs. He cried, "What did you do to me, Cody?"

I said, "I broke both your legs, you prick." He started begging for his life, and I told him to shut up as I went over and put a bullet in his left elbow, almost blowing his arm off. The bone shattered in pieces as the bullet entered his arm. It was now hanging by the skin and a few tendons. Blood and bone spattered everywhere as he screamed out louder in pain. I told him he didn't need to worry about the pain much longer because I would put him out of his misery in a little while.

I then grabbed Cori by her hair with my left hand while holding the gun in the other and dragged her into the bathroom. She was screaming and begging me the entire time not to kill her. As I held her up to the sink, I put her hand on the bathroom vanity cabinet and said, "So you liked touching that sorry piece of crap with your hands?" I took the butt of the pistol and smashed her fingers, breaking them into pieces. I then took her other hand and did the same thing.

I flipped the toilet's lid and then sat her down on it. I took a pair of scissors from the drawer and said to her, "You know what men from other countries do to their women when they commit adultery?" She didn't answer my question as she kept pleading with me to spare her life. I took the scissors and cut off her long, beautiful hair. I could hear the pain in her voice as she said, "I deserve this, Cody, but if you stop now, we can watch my hair grow back together." At that point, I was so out of control that it looked like what some little kid would do to their hair if they were left alone with a pair of scissors when I finished the cutting. It looked ridiculous, but at that point, that's just what I wanted.

I carried her back-limp body into the bedroom and threw her on the floor beside Bruce. I yelled at Bruce, "Look at her. How do you like the bitch now, you piece of crap?" I grabbed him by the hair and lifted his head so that he could see her. All I could hear from him was pathetic whimpering, and just like Cori, he was pleading for his life.

I told them how they committed the ultimate betrayal anyone could ever do to me. I said, "I knew something was happening when I caught you together in Texarkana. I should've killed you both then, especially after you made me feel and look like a fool." I got in Bruce's face and told him, "I warned you several times that I would kill anyone I caught with my wife. Why didn't you listen to me, you stupid, arrogant prick?"

He said in a choppy voice, "I couldn't help it, Cody. I fell in love with her."

Hearing those words outraged me even more. I went over and shot Bruce in the other elbow. Now he had both elbows just hanging by skin and tendons. He screamed out again, and that's just what I wanted to hear. I told him, "You should have stuck to the man code, you dummy, "YOU DON'T SCREW AROUND WITH YOUR BEST FRIEND'S WIFE." "She was off-limits, and you knew it. YOU DIDN'T LISTEN TO ME. Did you think you could get away with sneaking around with her?" I screamed at them, "Do you think having sex with each other was worth dying for?"

I was shouting at Bruce as I said, "We have had private and intimate talks about our wives. You knew how much I loved Cori and that she was MY WOMAN. Did you think I would give her to you and walk away? You should've stayed away from her." I went over and kicked him a couple of times in the ribs with my boots. He was bleeding all over the floor, and I knew he would bleed to death soon, and I didn't want that to happen. I like that the last thing he saw before he died was me pulling the trigger and putting a bullet in his head.

I made Cori watch all the pain he was going through and simultaneously suffered her own. She had blood running down her head. Her lip split open again, and it was bleeding. I calmly asked her,

"Didn't you believe me when I told you I would kill you if I ever caught you with another man?"

She wrenched in pain as she said, "Yes, but I always thought you loved me enough that you would forgive me if I got caught."

I screamed at her, "You knew how much I loved you, how much it would hurt me, and you still did this anyway. You're just a cheating bitch."

She slowly breathed out, "I'm sorry, Cody. I didn't do it to hurt you. I'm sorry. Please, please, don't kill me."

I told them that if they had any prayers, they better start saying them now because they would both be dead soon. The entire time I was torturing them, it was almost like I was in a bad dream that wouldn't end. I was so pumped up from the adrenaline and anger that my heart felt like it would explode. I was breathing heavily, and I couldn't think straight. I felt like I was disoriented and disconnected from the person who was torturing them. Everything was a blur like I was on a fast-moving train. I was shouting at the top of my lungs. I was kicking and throwing things around. I let them suffer and plead for their lives for several minutes as I went back and forth from uncontrolled anger to complete calm.

I went over to Bruce and kicked him in the ribs several times. I was so angry that I kicked Cori in the back. I knew that I wouldn't leave them that way, and I didn't want Bruce to bleed to death. I desperately wanted to put a bullet in him. They were like wounded deer. I had to put them out of their misery. I also had to finish the promise I had made myself when I was young.

I went to Bruce and said, "I thought you were my best friend. I hope you rot in hell." I lifted his head by his hair as I had him look at me and put a bullet right between his eyes. I then went to Cori and said, "Are you happy now? The cheating fucker is all yours. You can have his sorry ass because you deserve each other. I loved and trusted you above anyone else in the world. You made me feel like a fool! Now, you can join your lover, you cheating bitch. I held up her head to look at me as I pulled the trigger.

After it was over, I sat down on the bed and watched as part of her brain started oozing out of her head. She was still breathing, but I knew it wouldn't be long before she would be dead. It was over, and the cheaters wouldn't hurt me ever again. I looked around the room, at the hair, blood, and pieces of bone everywhere, and the two bodies in front of me. I thought THESE TWO CHEATING LOVERS DESERVED WHAT THEY GOT.

I sat there for a while. I realized the consequences of what I had just done. I panicked and ran out to my truck to head out of town. I didn't know what I was doing or where I was going. All I knew was that I wouldn't stick around and wait with their bodies for someone to find us together.

In my crazy, mixed-up state of mind, I decided to go to Little Rock and see my mom and let her know I had killed Cori and Bruce.

Three hours later, when I got there, she told me that she had already received a call from Jason and heard what had happened. He said the police told him when Carolyn Waters, the girl Cori rode to work with, went by to pick up Cori for work. She saw Bruce's car out front. She couldn't get anyone to answer when she knocked on all the doors. Not getting an answer, Carolyn went to the back, noticed it was open, and then went in. She found both Cori and Bruce's bodies lying on the floor in the main bedroom in puddles of blood. She called the police and then waited outside until they arrived.

The police looked over the crime scene and asked Carolyn who she thought might do something horrific. She said the only person she knew that would do something this gruesome was Cori's husband, Sherriff Cody Walker. She noted that Cori told her on the way to work, just the day before, that Cody had found out Cori and Bruce were having an affair. She said that Cody was outraged and told her he would kill them both. Carolyn told the police that Cody became so angry that he hit Cori and split her lip a few days earlier. She said it was the first time Cody had been violent with her. Cori told her that he had gone into the bedroom. Cody got some clothes and guns and left. He said he needed time to think about things, so he headed to California. Cori told her she knew Cody would kill her and Bruce the first chance he got and that it was just a matter of time. Carolyn told the police that Cody would be her first guess, but he was supposed to go to California."

***

Chapter 22 – Turning Myself in

The police put out an A.P.B. for my arrest, saying I was armed and dangerous. That wasn't true. Just because I had killed Cori and Bruce didn't mean I wanted to kill anyone else. I didn't feel like anyone else had done anything to me to deserve to die. I spent a few hours vacillating about what I should do at my mom's house. I kept listening to my mom telling me to return to Broken Arrow and turn myself in. She said I should face the consequences of what I'd done. My brain told me to run, but I didn't know where.

After going back and forth on what to do, I decided to go back and turn myself in. Before I left, I told my mom where I hid the $10,000.00 and told her to get it. I told her I needed to hire a lawyer for my defense. I told her to hang onto it until I had to give it to my lawyer once I found out who it would be. I told her I could be locked up for a long time unless I could convince a judge, jury, and everyone else of my version of what happened. I told her the only attorney I knew was Michael Jones of Queensland." I asked her to call him and let him know I was turning myself in and asking him to represent me. Little did I know he was the deputy prosecuting attorney working against me in my trial.

After saying my goodbyes to my mom, I returned to my pick-up and Broken Arrow. On the drive back, I tried to remember if the plan I had thought through so carefully beforehand would even work once I started piecing it together. It still made sense in my mixed-up and unstable frame of mind. I kept rehearsing my version of the story back. On the way back, I disposed of the gun I had used to kill them. I don't know why I did that. I wasn't planning to deny that I was the one that killed them. I wasn't thinking clearly.

I entered the city limits of Broken Arrow at about 9:45 pm. I was immediately pulled over and arrested by Douglas Fairbanks, one of the local police officers. He had his pistol pulled and aimed toward me, and he was shouting orders at me to get out of the pick-up and lie down on the ground. He treated me like I was another common criminal, and I did as he said. From my position, lying face down on the asphalt, I said, "Hey Doug, it's me, Sherriff Cody. You don't have to worry; I won't resist arrest." He didn't say anything; he cuffed me and threw me in his squad car.

I knew exactly how other people felt when they broke the law, and I had arrested them. I was nothing more than a killer to him. I was the low-life scumbag everyone talked trash about in our morning meetings.

On the drive to the police station, I had a compelling need to tell my version of what had happened to Officer Fairbanks. He told me I shouldn't say anything until my attorney was present. I knew I had to tell my story to someone to see if it made any sense and was believable. If Doug believed it, I figured maybe I had a chance that other people would.

I ignored his warnings not to say anything and started telling him my version of the story. "I told him that I did kill Bruce Tuttle, but it was in self-defense and that while shooting at him, I accidentally shot my wife Cori and killed her. I told him that the day before all this happened, Cori and I had a huge fight. I would stay in California for a while to get my head together. I was ready for Arizona when I realized that running away from my problems was a bad idea. I returned to Broken Arrow to see if we could work through our marriage. I arrived around the middle of the afternoon and noticed Bruce's car in front of my house. I drove down my driveway and got out of my truck. I went to the front door, locked it, went around to the back, unlocked it, and went in. I met Cori coming out of the main bedroom and adjusting her skirt. I asked her what was happening, and she said, "You don't want to know." After arguing with her for a few minutes, she admitted that she was with Bruce, and they had been having sex. I slapped her, knocking her against the wall and busting her lip. I told Cori it was over between us and went to my truck to get my suitcase and put more things in it.

When I returned to the house, I noticed Cori's split lip was bleeding, so I took her to the bathroom to help clean her up. We then discussed making amends with each other; all would be forgiven and forgotten. That's when she admitted that she had been having sex with Bruce for several months. At that point, I lost it and shoved her against the wall, which injured her head. When I saw what I did, I apologized again for hurting her and causing the cut on her head. Because the amount on her head wouldn't stop bleeding, I took her to the bathroom sink. I got a pair of scissors and started to cut the hair away from the wound. While trying to get all the hair away from the gash, I flashed back to a movie I'd recently seen. A woman accused of adultery had been publicly humiliated by having all her hair chopped off as a symbol of her sin. I told Doug that Cori didn't say a word as I cut chunks of her hair until the last bit fell to the floor. That's when she whispered, "It's okay, Cody, now we can watch it grow back together." I left Cori in the bathroom to sweep up the mess and entered our bedroom. I found Cori had left her handgun lying on a nightstand. I chastised her for leaving her gun around where a child could get a hold of it, and she nodded in agreement.

She finished sweeping her hair, so we went back to the bedroom so she could change out of her bloodied shirt when I heard a noise. At first, I thought it was a big dog, but it was Bruce coming at me with a knife instead. He'd been hiding in the closet. I fired warning shots over his head, but one of them grazed the top of his head. I told him to leave, or he would be a dead S.O.B. He acted as if he would go and then hesitated because the wound to his head dazed him. He then came at me again with a knife, and I fired 3 or 4 more times. I believe only 2 of the bullets hit Bruce, but I saw that one of the stray bullets must have hit Cori. She was lying on the floor, and at first, I thought she had just fainted until I tried to lift her head and realized bits of her brain were coming out because of the headshot. I went to Bruce and put a bullet in his head to ensure he wouldn't come after me again. I panicked, left the house, and drove up to Little Rock when I finally realized the severity of what I had done. I had gone to my mom's house, and she told me she'd heard what had happened and convinced me to return to Broken Arrow and turn myself in."

My version of the story made a lot of sense to me. It sounded like the whole thing could have just been a case of self-defense and an accident. It probably would've worked if it hadn't been for how I tortured them before I killed them. They each had broken bones throughout their bodies, in addition to the bullet wounds.

Douglas Fairbanks didn't seem to care about my side of the story as he took me straight to jail.

***

Chapter 23 - My Appeal

They charged me with "capital murder for having caused the deaths of two people with the deliberate and premeditated purpose of causing the death of a person."

I told my defense attorney that it was an accident and self-defense, but I knew what had happened in my heart. He asked me, "If that's the case, why were they so brutally tortured before they died?" I said, "I don't know what you're talking about?" He replied, "The way you had allegedly killed them by breaking each of their legs, all her fingers, shooting Bruce Tuttle in both elbows, and cutting off all of Cori's hair didn't corroborate the way you described it to everyone. The police could never find a knife on or near Bruce Tuttle." I said, "Maybe I went a little insane when I was killing them." He said, "Not just a little. You've got to be kidding me! If you would've just gone into the house and killed them and not tortured them, then, MAYBE, your story would fly with the court." He agitated me but said, "Don't worry; I'll do the best with what I've got to work with and see what we can do to get you off these charges."

A few days after I was locked up in the city jail, they let Jason come in to talk to me. I told him my version of what had happened and repeatedly told him I was sorry for killing his mom. I didn't tell him that I was still very angry with the two of them and believed they both got what they deserved. We cried a few times, and I told him I was sorry to leave him alone. I told him he was now on his own, and from that point, he would have to make all his own decisions. He was almost 17 by then, so it wasn't like he was just a little kid. We talked for several minutes, and I think he was trying hard to grasp everything that had happened. He was like me, still very angry with Bruce for all this happening to his mom. I told him my attorney would try to get me off the charges.

My mom and brothers came to see me in jail, and I told them the same story I told the police and Jason. I suggested that story so many times that I was starting to believe it! I even wrote letters to a few of my relatives and gave them my version of what happened. Even if it wasn't true, that version made me feel better and helped me accept what I had done.

I didn't see Kathy or the girls again until we were in Court. When they came in, I could see the pain on their faces. The girls were hurt and angry that I had killed their dad, but there was nothing I could do to ease their pain. I knew that even though Kathy was unhappy with Bruce, she still didn't want him dead. When I saw them, I tried not to look at them. I knew there was no point in making excuses or saying I was sorry (which I wasn't). He'd deceived me and made me feel like I was his best friend, but, according to Cori, it wasn't true. I was very pleased with myself for killing him.

While in prison, I remembered when I took Jason's deer hunting and fishing trips. I couldn't help but think of some of the bad things that had happened to me while growing up. I knew this place would eventually drive me crazier than I already was.

I appealed the verdict and brought up several errors or items of the trial that I thought were relevant to my case. What did I have to lose? I would be in prison for the rest of my life, so I didn't have anything else to do with my time. I figured there might even be some loophole to get me set free.

***

Chapter 24 - Time in Prison

After the sentence, I was handcuffed, shackled, and taken to Little Rock Prison to serve a sentence. Now, my new family would be armed robbers, thieves, and murderers like myself. Upon arrival at the prison facility, I processed at R & D (receiving and discharge). I was in a private holding cell with no other prisoners. They did fingerprint, photo processing, and an in-depth written questionnaire. I found out later that the questionnaire was placed in my file and used for evaluation by the psychologists and security staff. After processing, I was in an eight-by-ten cell. It had a toilet, sink, and bunk, and that was it.

I wasn't allowed phone privileges or mail during the first ten days. During that time, the division staff members interviewed me. Because I had been in law enforcement, they felt I had a safety issue. I had a target on my back. They decided to keep me isolated and not a member of the general prison population. I could take only two showers per week. I was issued four towels, four washcloths, four pairs of underwear, four pairs of socks, four uniform pants, four uniform shirts, four tee shirts, one pair of boots, a belt, a pillow, a pillowcase, two sheets, one blanket, and a laundry bag. I also issued two soap bars, two small tubes of toothpaste, a small toothbrush, two plastic razors, and two toilet paper rolls. I could replenish soap, toothpaste, razors, and toilet tissue twice weekly. I could exchange towels and washcloths twice a week and my blanket once a month. It was an oppressive and humiliating place to be. I wondered how I would survive in a place like this for the rest of my life.

A group of inmates was raping, the biggest thing I was worried about when I got to prison. If they tried to touch me, I would fight to protect myself. I soon found out the inmates targeted for abuse were either child molesters or young, naïve, shy, and first-time offenders. I knew I was a good fighter and could handle myself if I were in with the general prison population.

I found that being in Prison was almost like being a tribe member. Most inmates quickly aligned themselves with a group for protection. I didn't have to worry about it for the most part because I was kept in isolation most of the time. The only time I came out of my cell was for meals, watching television in one of the recreation rooms, or playing the guitar in the music room. I also could spend time at the prison library.

After a few years, I asked for and received a job in the laundry facility, and I worked there for 8 hours a day. I got a small amount to pay for a few things I wanted and needed. The prison life was dull and lonely, and I spent most of my time when I wasn't working daydreaming about Cori and my life before I went to prison.

I was in prison in Little Rock for the rest of my life. I settled in and realized I would never see the outside world again. Over the years, I spent hours with different psychiatrists, going over the murders, childhood, and every aspect of my life. I guess they were trying to figure out how a person of the law who appeared to be so "soft-spoken" and "easy-going" could've killed the people he supposedly cared for and loved the most. Maybe they were trying to rehabilitate me?

***

Chapter - 25 - My Final Plan

The years went by so slowly in prison that it felt like I was in a slow-motion movie. I hated prison life, and I sometimes wished I would get sick and die, have a heart attack or cancer, anything to get me out of the hell I was going through. At that point, I had been in prison for 12 years and was in my mid 50's.

I had nightmares every night, without fail. They were always the same and always about Cori. They began with the happy times of our marriage. When we were crazy in love with each other and unbelievably comfortable, it always ended up with me quickly turning dark, yelling at her and Bruce after catching them together in our bed. I would scream that she got what she deserved, reliving the torture I had inflicted upon them.

That happened the night the guard walked over to my cell and said, "Hey Cody, wake up. You're having that same dream again." I would always wake up exhausted and soaking wet from sweat. I constantly pulled out fresh clothes to change into; I couldn't help but think of how exhausting these dreams had become. They've taken a toll on my brain and my body. The daily battle of guilt versus justification for what I had done played out in a recurring fight of good against evil. At times, the blame was so overwhelming that it was all I could think about, and at other times, the anger and feelings of betrayal would surface, and anyone or anything within reach could become another victim. It was all just becoming too much for me.

I was always tired, rarely smiled, and felt I had little left to live for in this life. Then, I devised a plan to stop this endless cycle of self-torture. I made up my mind that I would get myself killed by one of the prison inmates. Several times, I met with some prison staff and told them I thought I'd be safe out in the general prison population since I'd been here so long. I told them I didn't believe I'd be a target after all the years. After much pleading and persuading, I finally convinced them to release me into the general prison population.

It didn't take long to realize that Truman Jones was the biggest and the meanest guy here. He was also the leader of the black gangs in prison. Truman was serving a couple of life terms for murder. I found out he always had someone to do his dirty work. If they didn't do what Truman told them, they would be the next on his list. I'd been around many scary people before, but he was one of the worst. Truman was just the guy I was looking for to do the job on me. He and his "homies" had nothing to lose if they killed someone. While in the general population yard, I studied his every move for the next few months.

I watched how his thugs attacked inmates with just a nod. They made shanks (knives or weapons) out of anything they could handle. I thought the best way to get this guy after I was to insult him and let the prison inmates know that I used to be a County Sheriff. After a few weeks of poking and prodding him, it started to work. He had guys that were beginning to torment me. They would try their best to bump into me whenever they could. On one occasion, one of his guys tried to take my food at lunch, and I threw my entire plate in his face. He jumped me, started punching the guards, and I broke it up. They put me in solitary confinement for a few days and then turned me loose after I promised it wouldn't happen again.

I started calling Truman and his thugs names and insulted them every chance I got. I called them punks and other derogatory names. I knew these guys were getting tired of me, and they wouldn't let me get away with it much longer. I knew it wouldn't be long before they decided they had had enough of my insults and killed me.

One night, I sat on my bunk and talked to what I thought was Cori. I told her that I would be seeing her soon. Even though I believed she deserved what she got for cheating on me, I still loved her and the memories we shared before the affair started. Now, none of that mattered anymore. I was tired of the torture I was putting myself through and wanted it all to end.

The next day, I was walking alone in the yard when I spotted Truman. I walked over to him, called him a few choice names, and then walked away. In a few minutes, a couple of his thugs came up behind me. One of them started stabbing me with his shank. I didn't try to fight back because that was just what I wanted. The other guy joined in the stabbing as I fell to the ground. At first, I felt the pain when the shank went deep into my chest. I could tell one of them had pierced my heart, and I knew my life would be over soon. At that point, I couldn't feel anything, and everything around me started to go black. I was gasping for my last breath, and the last thing I could remember seeing as I lay there dying was the image of Cori. I smiled and softly said, "I Love you, Cori."

***

Cody's last plan had worked.

A prison psychiatrist obtained all accounts of his life story while Cody sat there.

***

Corinne S. Walker died on December 28, 1988, at her husband, Cody D. Walker. She was 35 years old.

Bruce D. Tuttle died on December 28, 1988, at the hands of Cody D. Walker. He was 38 years old.

Cody D. Walker died in the Little Rock State Prison on June 22, 2000. He was killed by fellow inmates while serving only 12 years of his life sentence. He was 55 years old.

Jason had difficulty accepting Cori's death and lived with his biological father in California.

Several years after Bruce's death, Kathy Tuttle remarried and lives on the little farm in Broken Arrow, Arkansas.

***

Special Thanks

I want to give special thanks to my daughter, Danielle Nicole Derby Carter, for helping me with the computer work on this book.

I want to give a huge thanks to my ex-wife, Tami.

I would also like to thank Susan (Sue) Derby Marshall for editing the book.

***

Other books by Ron L. Carter
Twenty-One Months
Unearthly Realms
The American Terrorist – A Grandfather's Revenge
The American Terrorist – The Revenge Continues
The American Terrorist – The Silent Killer
Night Crawlers
Night Crawlers – Reign of Terror
Night Crawlers – The Nightmares Continue
Accidental Soldiers
Zak Thomas – The Monster Hunter
In Defense of Mankind
Ignited
Love me now, Don't wait – Poetry
Zak Thomas – The Moster Hunter
Lost Waters